MS. HOLMES & MS. WATSON – APT. 2B

BY KATE HAMILL

CHEERFULLY DESECRATING THE STORIES OF SIR ARTHUR CONAN DOYLE

MS. HOLMES & MS. WATSON - APT. 2B
Copyright © 2023 Kate Hamill
ALL RIGHTS RESERVED

COPYRIGHT NOTICE:
This Play is fully protected under the copyright laws of the United States of America and all countries covered by the International Copyright Union (including the British Commonwealth, Canada, Australia), the Berne Convention, the Pan-American Copyright Convention, and the Universal Copyright Convention, as well as all countries throughout the world with which the United States has reciprocal copyright relations. All rights, including but not limited to professional, amateur, and educational stage rights, motion picture, recitation, lecturing, public reading, radio broadcasting, television, video, YouTube, Zoom or any such Internet service or transmission, or sound recording, all other forms of mechanical or electronic reproduction, such as CD-ROM, CD-I, DVD, information storage and retrieval systems and photocopying, and the rights of translation into foreign languages, are strictly reserved. No part of this book may be reproduced, or transmitted in any form, by any means, now known or yet to be invented, without the prior written permission of Theatrical Rights Worldwide in its capacity as publisher.

SPECIAL NOTE ON SONGS AND RECORDINGS:
For the performance of copyrighted songs, arrangements or recordings as mentioned or contained in this Play, the permission of the copyright owner(s) must be obtained by You prior to their use. If You are unable to secure permission from the copyright owner(s), other songs, arrangements or recordings may be substituted provided You obtain permission from the copyright owner(s) of such songs, arrangements or recordings. Furthermore, songs, arrangements or recordings in the public domain, which are no longer governed by copyright and do not require permission for their use, may be substituted. Any substitution by You of the songs, arrangements or recordings as found in the Play must reflect the intention of the Author with respect to style, theme and content.

PERFORMANCE WARNING and ADVISORY:
Professional, amateur, and educational groups are hereby advised that performance of this Play requires a license and is subject to payment of a royalty whether or not admission is charged. The stage performance rights throughout the world for this Play are controlled exclusively by Theatrical Rights Worldwide. No professional, amateur, or educational performance may be given without obtaining, in advance of any and all

performances, the written permission of Theatrical Rights Worldwide and paying the requisite fee. Current royalty rates and performance information may be found at our website at www.theatricalrights.com and www.theatricalrights.co.uk. Inquiries concerning all other rights should be forwarded to:

Theatrical Rights Worldwide
1180 Avenue of the Americas, 6th Floor
New York, NY 10036
trwplays@theatricalrights.com

and

Theatrical Rights Worldwide
19 Margaret Street, 3rd Floor
London W1W 8RR UK
trwplays@theatricalrights.co.uk

THEATRICAL RIGHTS WORLDWIDE ATTRIBUTION:
Professional, amateur, and educational licensees shall include the following notice in all programs, advertisements, and other printed material distributed or published in connection with the production of the Play:

MS. HOLMES & MS. WATSON - APT. 2B
is produced by special arrangement with Theatrical Rights Worldwide.
www.theatricalrights.com
www.theatricalrights.co.uk

Printed in the U.S.A. / U.K.
ISBN: 978-1-63852-162-4

The world premiere production of *Ms. Holmes & Ms. Watson - Apt. 2B* was originally commissioned and produced by Kansas City Repertory Theatre; Stuart Carden, Artistic Director, on February 1st, 2022. It was directed by José Zayas; the associate director was Anna Sell; the scenic design was by Collette Pollard; the costume design was by Paul Kim; the lighting design was by Rachel Cady; the sound design was by Megan Culley; the wig design was by Gayla Voss; the fight director was Logan Black; the production stage manager was Emily White Winter, and the assistant stage manager was Rachel M. Dyer. The dramaturg was Hallie Gordon.

The cast was as follows (in alphabetical order):
Ms. Joan Watson .... KATE HAMILL
Inspector Lestrade, Elliot Monk, & Others .... JASON O'CONNELL
Irene Adler, Mrs. Hudson, & Others .... VANESSA SEVERO
Ms. Sherlock Holmes .... VAISHNAVI SHARMA

NOTE: The billing for the cast in programs should be exactly as it was for the world premiere, above. Please do NOT list Moriarty in any playbill or promotional materials... let him not be named until he is named in the play.

Character List
(3W, 1M)

SHERLOCK HOLMES / as cast *(30s-40s)*: female-identify in-a-generation genius. Eccentric. Focused, to a fault. Can b̲_ _̲ sensitive. Always playing psychological 3-D chess; operating on a totally different level than civilians. Like many geniuses, has a megalomaniac streak. Gets bored easily; likes applause; sometimes accused of being unfeeling. LOVES costumes and drama.

DR. JOAN WATSON / as cast *(30s-40s)*: female-identifying. American. Formerly type-A high-achiever. Recently divorced; struggling to find herself, feels broken. Reflexively defensive. Once had great bedside manner. Sometimes accused of being a loser; is not a loser. Wry. Smart.

IRENE ADLER / MRS. HUDSON / MRS. DREBBER / as cast *(late 20s-40s)*: female-identifying.
> <u>Irene Adler:</u> a whip-smart, super-charming sex worker finding success at the highest levels. Always playing psychological 3-D chess; operating on a totally different level than civilians. Has incredible charm, confidence, and wit, and she knows it—uses it without mercy. You may want to be Irene, or you may want to be *with* Irene; but you can't ignore her.
> <u>Mrs. Hudson:</u> Holmes & Watson's long-suffering landlady.
> <u>Mrs. Drebber:</u> seemingly an ordinary housewife. Somebody you would be very wise not to underestimate.

MORIARTY / LESTRADE / ELLIOT MONK / as cast *(30s-50s)*: male-identifying.
> <u>Moriarty:</u> a criminal so great you've never heard of him. A master blackmailer; knows just when to play his cards. Always playing psychological 3-D chess; operating on a different level than civilians. Wears many masks. A professional. Amoral, but you'd like him.
> <u>Lestrade:</u> an inspector new to his position at Scotland Yard. Not very imaginative. Often says the wrong thing.
> <u>Elliot Monk:</u> an amoral tech billionaire from Texas.

Setting

Today. And also spring 2021. Mostly set in London and the surrounding areas. Sometimes set in your theater, right now, right this moment—look, we're right behind you!

Playwright's Notes

It is not necessary to have big scene or costume changes. Much / most / all of the play's scenery can be created from the chaotic curios of Apt. 2B.... let the audience's imaginations fill in the gaps. It should be SUPER fun and fast, like kids playing dress-up out of a slightly macabre toy trunk. Also, it should get very messy.

- Please do not list Moriarty anywhere in your program notes or marketing materials – it ruins the surprise! In the world premiere, we listed the character as INSPECTOR LESTRADE, ELLIOT MONK, & OTHERS. Don't play the Moriarty card until you must!
- Re: the blood moment. The bigger the set-up, the bigger the corresponding pay-off must be. If there's a lot of prep, it's got to be a TON of blood. While I'm always pro-a-metric-ton-of-blood, I recommend as little prep as possible so the audience doesn't get too far ahead of the joke. And I really, really recommend costumes that can get bloody and stay bloody through intermission, or even the end of the play. This is just a messy one!
- The more excitement and fear and joy and general heightened stakes the actors feel, the more we'll go for the ride – especially if the pace is up, and especially if Holmes' energy is up when on the case. She almost never walks – she bounds. The guns in the pentultimate railway scene must be very, very present. I know it's a lot of twists and turns to get through, but keep that gun tension up.
- Perhaps there is a chess board onstage—from time to time, mid-scene without remarking on it, both the actors playing Holmes & Moriarty make moves upon it.
- It would be satisfying if the actors playing Holmes & Watson switched roles from night to night, but it is certainly not requisite.
- Any line said by Watson in [brackets] is said at half-volume; a throwaway line.
- Most of the characters have British accents; Watson, Elliot Monk, and the reporter are American. This play takes place in 2021, in London. Sherlock Holmes need not be British, but she is not

American. Moriarty has a Cockney accent; Lestrade does not have a Cockney accent.
- Dialogue should go fast, fast, fast, speed-of-thought fast. Often, faster than you think. And Sherlock, when deducing, goes faster still.

Note on Music Usage

In this play the author suggests using a song like "Bad Boys," "Put on A Happy Face," or "Milkshake" as a possible ring tone for the character LESTRADE's phone. As these are suggestions and are not required elements, the right to use any of these songs is not included as part of the right to produce the play. If you wish to use one of these songs or any other song or recording still protected under copyright laws in your production of *Ms. Holmes & Ms. Watson - Apt. 2B*, then you should obtain the proper permission from the copyright holder or their representative.

Dedicated to my siblings and their partners: Paul, Steve & Michele, Matt & Kelly, Rachel & Michael, Brendan & Harim. The best & loudest family imaginable.

PROLOGUE.

A stage. Yes, just a stage. Moriarty talks directly to the audience. As he does, the actors set up the scene behind him.

MORIARTY:
Hello, suckers.
It's good to be back, all together, isn't it? Good to watch, to listen in—to see the hidden revealed, even as you sit—anonymous—in the dark.
Anyhoo, unwrap your candies, turn off your phones—and prepare to be transported to the foggy streets of Ye Oldee London Towne, circa eighteen seventy—*(Actress 3 whispers in his ear)*
We're not? Can I ask *(why)*—*(she whispers in his ear)*
I know theaters are strapped right now, but budget isn't everything. *(she whispers in his ear)* Well, neither is "originality," and audiences have certain *expectations*—*(she whispers in his ear)* Really? And who is playing whom—*(she gestures)* Ooo, you are going to get some angry emails.
I have been informed that you will *not* be transported into the 19th century, this evening. Instead you'll be transported—to...today. Ish. Spring 2021. Sorry! This won't be a period piece, and I'm told that was made clear in the marketing materials. *(someone in the cast flashes a program)*
So—why are you here?

No, really. In a bewildering world, why come see more souls floundering in the unknowable?

I think I know your dirty little secret, Madame.
I think—you want—*solutions*.
I think what we find satisfying
About any detective story, be it ever so—"original"
Is the idea that there *are* indeed patterns behind—life's distressing mysteries.

That "everything happens for a reason."

But what if that's just a comforting illusion?
What if there are—no underlying reasons in this chaotic world,
No control of cause and effect?
<u>What if there are no answers.</u>
Not every question
Can be answered! not every piece will fit!
and some are just meant to be—losers in the game!!
Forever flailing, forever unmoored—losers much like <u>her.</u>

> *He has pointed out JOAN WATSON. She looks a mess. Wearing all-black: combat boots, hair in a messy bun. Chipped black nail polish. She rolls a beaten-up, small suitcase—half-peeled airplane stickers all over it.*

WATSON:
Hey—what the frig?!

> *to the audience*

I am not—a "loser!"
My life—is just—in transition.

MORIARTY:
Tell me, Madame—how long has it been since you held down a job?

WATSON:
I'm exploring new horizons.

MORIARTY:
How long since you had a date?

WATSON:
I'm focusing on my self right now!

MORIARTY:
How long since—*(evocatively sniffing)* whew, you took a shower?

WATSON:
—Back off.

MORIARTY:
So you're "not a loser"... but yet—you are lost.

WATSON:
Not anymore. Look! Here it is! 221 Baker Street. *(Watson hits a doorbell; ding, dong)* Now scram.

MORIARTY:
See you later—Watson.

WATSON:
Hey! Hey! How do you know my na—

ACT ONE

1.

The door opens; MRS. HUDSON, a landlady in her 60s, sticks her head out. Mrs. Hudson is, it must be said, VERY anxious.

MRS. HUDSON:
Hello?

Watson stares off towards where Moriarty went.

Can I help you, dear?

Watson shakes it off.

WATSON:
Yes. Yeah, sorry! Hi! Mrs. Hudson? I'm Joan Watson—we emailed.

MRS. HUDSON:
Oh! An American, are you?

WATSON:
Yup.

MRS. HUDSON:
Well, nobody's perfect.

WATSON:
Thanks.

MRS. HUDSON:
(she welcomes her in) As I said in my advert, Miss Watson—I'm looking for a month-to-month tenant for my upstairs flat—Number 2B. *(she hands her rental materials)*

WATSON:
The rent is *super* reasonable.

MRS. HUDSON:
I've been looking for some time—for the perfect match. But it's—it is not for everyone, I suppose! *(she drops her keys, nervously)* Some people are so picky!

WATSON:
And it's furnished, too?

MRS. HUDSON:

Bedroom, kitchen, and common area—but that's shared space.

WATSON:

"Shared"?

MRS. HUDSON:

(she drops her keys) I have one long-term tenant; afraid she's got squatter's rights, runs a small business out of the parlor.

WATSON:

What kind of business?

MRS. HUDSON:

(veering closer and closer to a nervous breakdown) Oh dear. It's all a bit over my head, and I always use the wrong words, and then she gets—fussy. *(she drops the keys)* But I'm sure she'll tell you all about it herself! *(she drops the keys)* She's ah—very keen! *(drops the keys)* On explanations! *(Mrs. Hudson has to hold the keys with both hands; they are nervously jangling)*

WATSON:

I'll probably keep to my bedroom a lot, anyways. I'm kind of—in a transitional phase right now. Doing some deep processing—trying out creative writing. Grounding—in some new truths.

MRS. HUDSON:

You know, dear, some say Americans are too open.

WATSON:

I just need a quiet place to get away.

Mrs. Hudson turns her keys in the door to enter #2B—

MRS. HUDSON:

Well—you should—*(suddenly, LOUD classical music switches on—Mrs. Hudson tries to soldier on)* you should certainly have that here—

WATSON:

/What is—?

MRS. HUDSON:

/Lord, she's on the Rachmaninoff again.

WATSON:

—is that COMING FROM YOUR TENANT

Mrs. Hudson opens the door, and the music is VERY loud indeed

MRS. HUDSON:

WHILE SHE MAY BE A BIT—ECCENTRIC, MS. WATSON—

she drops the keys as she pulls them back out of the door

WATSON:
> WHAT—

MRS. HUDSON:
> THEY SAY WE CANNOT JUDGE A BOOK'S CHARACTERS BY ITS COVER—

WATSON:
> WHAT?

MRS. HUDSON:
> OH BLOODY **HELL**

>> *They both enter the flat. Mrs. Hudson grabs a nearby broom and brandishes it like a weapon, afraid somebody might jump out at her.*

MRS. HUDSON:
> WILL YOU TURN DOWN THAT PONCY NONSENSE ALREADY! ALRIGHT THEN I'LL DO IT MYSELF! I'M TOUCHING THE DIAL!! I'M TURNING OFF THE RACHMANINOFF now

>> *She hits a button on the stereo—silence.*

> Oo I'll pay for that later.

WATSON:
> What—is happening?

>> *Mrs. Hudson holds the broom like a sword—points with trembling finger, towards a closed door.*

MRS. HUDSON:
> Nothing. Absolutely nothing! Ahahaha. Could you just—open that door for me, love?

>> *Watson opens the door, as Mrs. Hudson waves the broom frantically, her eyes squeezed tight.*

MRS. HUDSON:
> EEEEEAAAAAAA! DON'T JUMP OUT AT ME NOW DON'T DON'T DON'T!!

WATSON:
> Um—what?

MRS. HUDSON:
> Nothing. Never mind. *(she releases the broom)* So—this is the flat!

>> *Watson takes a real look at the apartment. It is ratty. A terrible college apartment meets a curio shop. Food wrappers strewn everywhere. A mix of incredibly strange period pieces and modern elements. Like a mad scientist and a teenager live there. Beakers and soda bottles. Leather-bound books and fashion magazines. Weapons and maps, but also puzzles and toys, half-dissected. A mini-fridge. A grungy coffee*

table, covered with newspapers and old meals. A beat-up couch. And centrally—a human skeleton.

WATSON:
Gosh, it is—a real fixer-upper, isn't it?

MRS. HUDSON:
But it's got good bones!

WATSON:
(poking at the skeleton) Yeah, I can see that.

MRS. HUDSON:
Should you like to see the bedroom?

Watson, with trepidation, nods / shrugs, makes a non-committal sound

Lovely. It's right through—

Mrs. Hudson reaches for a door—and Sherlock Holmes bursts through at her, in fencing mask and foil. The audience should think, for a moment, that Mrs. Hudson is genuinely being attacked.

HOLMES:
AHHHH!!!!!!

MRS. HUDSON:
AHHHHHHHHHH HHHH HHHHHH HHHHH

Mrs. Hudson brandishes the broom; Holmes quite handily evades the bristles.

WATSON:	**HOLMES:**
AHHHHH	AHHHHHHHHHHHHHHHHH

WATSON:
AHHHHH WHAT THE FRIG IS FRIGGING HAPPENING?!!!

HOLMES:
I'LL TELL YOU WHAT! An experiment is repeated—and yet the subject chooses the same response! If I've said it once, I've said it a hundred times, Mrs. Hudson! Never let them take you by surpr<u>EN GARDE!</u>

Holmes pounces towards Mrs. Hudson; she SCREAMS and ducks— Holmes whirls away

And it was NOT Rachmaninoff!

Holmes bounds back towards the stereo

It's Igor Fyodorovich Stravinsky!!!

Holmes presses play again—loud, high-energy, thumping, driving music plays

MRS. HUDSON:
MS. WATSON

HOLMES:
Not ALL RUSSIANS ARE THE SAME!

MRS. HUDSON:
MS. WATSON MAY I INTRODUCE—

HOLMES:
YOU'LL BE SAYING IT'S BY ANTON CHEKHOV NEXT!!!!

Mrs. Hudson slams the pause button; the music stops—and

MRS. HUDSON:
Ms. Shirley Holmes!

Sherlock removes her mask. She is dressed like a steampunk dream. A scientist's goggles on her head. Unruly hair, pulled back. An iconoclast. A genius. A bit of a mess. Holmes tosses her fencing mask on the couch; if it lands on the floor, she does not care.

HOLMES:
If I've told you once, woman, I've told you a thousand—it is not "Shirley". It's Sherlock.

MRS. HUDSON:
—really, what kind of a name is "Sherlock", dear?

HOLMES:
It's French—for "not Shirley".

WATSON:
Pleasure to meet you—Ms. Holmes. I'm Joan Watson. *(Watson sticks out her hand—Holmes eyes it.)*

HOLMES:
Mmm.—But ARE you—REALLY.

Holmes gets close—uncomfortably close.

WATSON:
[what]

MRS. HUDSON:
(with increasing desperation) Sherlock—do be nice to this one!

HOLMES:
An American, are you?

WATSON:
Yep.

HOLMES:
My condolences.

WATSON:
Thanks.

HOLMES:
And a New Yorker at that!

WATSON:
How do /you—

HOLMES:
All-black clothing, earbuds, reflexive hostility. Elementary.

WATSON:
"Elementary"?

HOLMES:
A child could figure it out.

MRS. HUDSON:
(desperately) Sherlock—be polite!!!

> *Holmes throws herself upon the sofa, puts her feet up on the coffee table, and moodily takes off her fencing gloves—throwing them on the floor.*

HOLMES:
Polite! POLITE!

MRS. HUDSON:
Please!!!

HOLMES:
I shall be exactly as *polite* as any other great craftsman who finds that their life's work has become meaningless! Would you hector the heartbroken to smile, Mrs. Hudson. Would you ask the bereavéd to dance a jig?!!

WATSON:
Should I—come at another time?

HOLMES:
There is no good time for me, now. There shall be no good time, ever again!

MRS. HUDSON:
She's not always like this, Ms. Watson!

WATSON:
No?

MRS. HUDSON:
No! Sometimes she's manic!

WATSON:
Yeah—I think I'm gonna take off.

Watson begins to leave.

MRS. HUDSON:
Damn it, Sherlock, you've frightened away another one!

HOLMES:
I told you that I didn't want a flatmate!

MRS. HUDSON:
It's not healthy, you cooped up all alone! No man is an island!

HOLMES:
(creating chaos) Good thing I AM NO MAN! *(banging things, bang bang bang)*

WATSON:
So, um, peace out everyone. Be seeing you never!

HOLMES:
(as Watson opens the door to go) Lovely to meet you—Doctor Watson!

Watson freezes at the door.

WATSON:
Uh—I am not a doctor.

HOLMES:
Yes, you are.

WATSON:
No, I'm not.

Watson comes back into the room.

HOLMES:
Yes you are.

WATSON:
No I'm not.

| **HOLMES:** | **WATSON:** |
| Yes you are yes you are yes you are yes you are— | No I'm not no I'm not no I'm not NO I'M !!! |

MRS. HUDSON:
This is going well.

HOLMES:
YOU CANNOT DISPUTE THE EVIDENCE—Doctor!

WATSON:
What "evidence"?

MRS. HUDSON:
Here we go.

Holmes plies her craft; she is not afraid to get into Watson's personal space. EVERY time Holmes gives her deduction summaries throughout the play, they are VERY fast—the other characters, and the audience, should barely keep up.

HOLMES:
—elementary.
You hold the rental materials close, sideways, like a clipboard—shielding them even from Mrs. Hudson: exercising reflexive doctor-patient confidentiality, as you are accustomed to holding medical charts!

WATSON:
Lots of people hold their papers sideways!

HOLMES:
Your hands are meticulously clean—under the nails and up to the wrist; textbook medical hand-washing procedure! What's more, the skin is dry, rough—it's been years of such habits, a decade of scrubbing up!

WATSON:
Um, it's post-2020, lady. Lots of people have very clean hands.

HOLMES:
Ah, but those spic-and-span sanitized hands keep reaching to your upper neck; as if adjusting a stethoscope! Your watch—an expensive model, though wearing at the band, and unusually—featuring a pulsometer; a med school graduation present, perhaps?!

WATSON:
—lots of people wear WATCHES!

HOLMES:
And finallemente—chorus, crescendo, *IL CULMINE*—
Your luggage tag.

Holmes points at the offending tag.

WATSON:
It—it doesn't say anything but "Joan Watson!"

HOLMES:
Does it really?
The handwriting is entirely incomprehensible.
You might as well be wearing scrubs—Doctor.

MRS. HUDSON:
(*applauding wildly*) Bravo, oh, bravo, brava!!!! You see, Doctor Watson—

WATSON:
Ms! I'm telling you, you're *wrong*.

MRS. HUDSON:
You have now witnessed the work of Sherlock Holmes, internationally celebrated detective!

HOLMES:
I much prefer "deductive consultant".

MRS. HUDSON:
(just trying to make the sale, speed it up) Whatever—

HOLMES:
Professional hypothesizer, if you must.

MRS. HUDSON:
Whatever—

HOLMES:
I root out that which would remain hidden—inevitably accomplishing the improbable—if not the impossible!

MRS. HUDSON:
Whatever, whatever!—you must have heard of her pre-pandemic exploits?! *(acting these out vividly)* The Case of The Creeping Man? The Adventure of The Sussex Vampire? The Consumption of Lady Carfax's Corpse?

WATSON:
Those all sound very made-up.

MRS. HUDSON:
—well, perhaps she is not widely known in America, where nobody reads. But she may be the most accomplished "deductive consultant"... in the world!

HOLMES:
CORRECTION: I was. *Was.* A deservedly celebrated iconoclast, Mrs. Hudson. Now I am—adrift. Wrung dry. Washed up.
"Alexander wept, for there were no more worlds to conquer."

MRS. HUDSON:
She means Alexander the Great.

WATSON:
Yeah, I've seen *Die Hard.*

HOLMES:
Crime has become so—quotidian. Law-breakers have no imagination anymore! Every day, just—murder, robbery, assault. Murder, robbery assault. Murder murder death and murder—blah blah blahblahblahblah BLAH.

WATSON:
Yikes.

HOLMES:
My fire has burned out. I have lost all inspiration!

MRS. HUDSON:
Oh, Sherlock. Buck up.

> *She starts singing:*

Grey skies are gonna clear up, put on a happy face— /strike up the band

HOLMES:
(grimacing as Mrs. Hudson keeps going under) /I am alone, <u>alone</u> in my anguish. There is nothing left... but escape.

> *From the recesses of the coffee table, Holmes finds a little baggie of marijuana, and a pipe. Her pipe must be noticeably for weed—not tobacco.*

WATSON:
Whoa.—is that—?!!

HOLMES:
Relax. It's legal, now. Mostly.

> *Holmes lights herself a bowl of weed, and takes a big hit.*

WATSON:
It's also the middle of the day.

HOLMES:
(holding her breath) What is day, when all is night?

MRS. HUDSON:
Ooo, Sherlock—open a window

HOLMES:
It's what artists do—when the muse goes mute.

MRS. HUDSON:
—have you disabled the smoke alarm again?

HOLMES:
Van Gogh cut off his ear! Picasso hopped from bed to bed! Michelangelo took to robbing graves!

MRS. HUDSON:
(wagging her finger, cheerily) I'll have to fine you!

HOLMES:
Sherlock Holmes—seeks slight solace in chemical sedative!
(taking up the foil again) Physical restorative! And should that fail—
Pyotr Ilyich Tchaikovsky!

> *Holmes hits the button again—the loud, thump-y portion of the 1812 Overture plays*

MRS. HUDSON:
Another Russian, Sherlock!!!

HOLMES:
POLISH, MRS. HUDSON! MY GOD WOMAN, WE HAVE TO TRAIN YOUR EAR!

Holmes bounces around, fencing the air:

MRS. HUDSON:
SO—DOCTOR WATSON—

WATSON:
MS. /—

MRS. HUDSON:
WHEN SHALL YOU MOVE IN

Holmes bounds across the room with her foil, mock-attacking Watson:

HOLMES:
SALUTE, DOCTOR

WATSON:
ACTUALLY

HOLMES:
ADVANCE

WATSON:
MRS. HUDSON

HOLMES:
PARRY

WATSON:
I THINK I NEED TO LOOK AT OTHER

HOLMES:	**MRS. HUDSON:**
RIPOSTE!	SHIRLEY WILL YOU
RIPOSTE! RIPOSTE!	TURN DOWN (THAT)

WATSON:
OH FOR THE LOVE OF—

Watson storms over to turn off the stereo herself—and gets in the way of Holmes' pounce.

HOLMES:
EN GAR—

Watson accidentally smacks Holmes in the face. Holmes reels.

WATSON:
Ahh! I'm—/ sorry, but you were in the—

MRS. HUDSON:
/Sherlock!

> *Holmes is bleeding, slightly, from her nose. She shrugs it off cheerfully—but Watson sags, weak at the knees.*

HOLMES:
"A touch, a touch, I do confess!" Nice strong backhand, Watson, could come in helpful in a—Watson?

> *Watson is bent over, her breath coming short.*

MRS. HUDSON:
Are you all right, dear? *(Watson can't respond; she pats her back, but Watson flinches away. A long beat.)* Heavens... what brought this on?

WATSON:
I don't know. What causes it, exactly—it comes and goes. Just—give me a sec. *(she hangs her head between her knees)*

HOLMES:
A doctor who can't see blood.

WATSON:
I said I'm not a doctor!!!

> *Beat.*

MRS. HUDSON:
Well. *(to Holmes)* What. A. Mystery!

HOLMES:
(captivated) HaaaaAAAaaahhhh.

> *Holmes stares at Watson; Watson's head is still between her own knees.*

WATSON:
Mrs. Hudson,—this situation—is not the best fit for me. Don't you have anything else?

MRS. HUDSON:
Not at this rent.

HOLMES:
And you need this, badly—don't you, Watson.

WATSON:
What?

> *She looks up at Holmes' bleeding nose, immediately has to drop her head*

HOLMES:
Your shoes. Doc Martens, bit young for you, aren't they? Paired with the black nail polish—you're trying to recapture better days—start

over—but your cuticles are ragged; you've been biting them from anxiety. Then there's the luggage, covered with travel stickers—bouncing from place to place—but only for a few weeks each time—downgrading from first class to economy to practically hanging onto the tail-fins. And here—ah—the tan line from a wedding ring, but no ring is evident.

MRS. HUDSON:
Are you doing a sort of *Eat Pray Love*, dear?

WATSON:
You're just guessing. Randomly!

MRS. HUDSON:
I didn't care for that movie.

HOLMES:
I'm just hypothesizing. Expertly.

MRS. HUDSON:
Julia Roberts. So *horsey*.

HOLMES:
You're running from something, Watson—but it's catching up—isn't it?

Holmes no longer bleeds; Watson tries to stand.

WATSON:
None of this—is any—of your business.

HOLMES:
You are a puzzle that needs to be solved. It is *implicitly* my business.

MRS. HUDSON:
Now *Sisterhood of the Traveling Pants*, that's a film.
America Ferrera.
So much charm.

HOLMES:
.....Congratulations, Doctor! I will take the case!

WATSON:
Excuse me???

HOLMES:
The mystery of Watson, the origin of your miserable psychological affliction, the demon that keeps you running! Oh, I feel ALIVE AGAIN!

WATSON:
No no no no—

HOLMES:

I'll take you on pro-bono. But you'll need close observation—which is why it is indeed convenient for you to move in immediately—

WATSON:

No no no no—

Holmes bounds over to the stereo.

HOLMES:

And THAT——THAT calls for Rachmaninoff!

The music is not quite as loud. Holmes plays air violin to it, energetically, as:

MRS. HUDSON:

Seems as though you've just made a friend, dear.

WATSON:

No no no no no NO. NO. NO—

MRS. HUDSON:

A roommate, then.

HOLMES:

Really, Watson. *(suddenly in quite close to her)*—Aren't you seeking a solution?

Watson stares at her, opens her mouth—Holmes releases her and bounds across the room

HOLMES:

EN GARDE! RIPOSTE! PARRY! THRUST!

2.

A few days later. The apartment. Watson walks out, holding a whole, jointed human finger bone. Holmes is clipping her toenails on the couch.

WATSON:
Holmes—hi, good morning. I was just, um, putting away my toothbrush, and in my holder, I found,—this?

HOLMES:
Ah! I wondered where that had gone!

WATSON:
Yeah. Is it—is it a finger?

HOLMES:
Look who's making deductions, now!

WATSON:
Is it—is it real?

HOLMES:
It has mass, weight, dimension, Watson. It is obviously real.

Holmes takes the finger. Watson reaches for a mug of coffee, considering:

WATSON:
Umhm, umhm, right. I meant—*(sips coffee)*—was that once attached to a living human bei—

HOLMES:
STOP! Watson—you didn't put creamer in that coffee, did you? From the fridge?

WATSON:
No, what—why?

HOLMES:
Good. Do not use the creamer.

WATSON:
....why?!

HOLMES:
You shouldn't be eating my food anyhow!

WATSON:
Holmes. Why no creamer?!!!

HOLMES:
Nothing. No reason.
—I am in the midst of some minor experiments.

Watson stares at her—Holmes finally concedes

It may contain the teeniest tiniest bit of arsenic.

Watson frantically scrubs her tongue.

WATSON:
AhhhHHHHHhhhh!

HOLMES:
I *knew* it.

WATSON:
Am I going to die?!!

HOLMES:
No, no, no. Probably not. Let me know if your tongue goes numb.

Watson spits and puts down her coffee.

HOLMES:
In fact, you really should stay away from every dairy product. Just to be safe.

WATSON:
—are they all poisoned?!!!

HOLMES:
No, Watson. You have a spot of lactose intolerance!

WATSON:
How do you—nope, nope, never mind. Not taking the bait.

Watson starts cleaning, angrily. Holmes plays with the finger—gives her the finger with it.

HOLMES:
Hey—Watson. You're number one. Hoo hoo! I'm literally giving you the finger! Get it?! Hee hee!

WATSON:
Hilarious. Shouldn't you be—doing something slightly more productive right now?

HOLMES:
Like what?

WATSON:
You said you were this big deal supersleuth. Shouldn't you be out—chasing bloodhounds, or something?

HOLMES:
When you're a clever enough mousetrap—the rodents must eventually come to you.

WATSON:
Yeah, um, speaking of rodents—maybe we could pick up this place a bit? Yknow, just before—the city has it condemned.

HOLMES:
<u>OR</u> you could sit down, have a lovely smoke—

WATSON:
Let's make a chore wheel!

HOLMES:
—and tell me all about your debilitating panic attacks and from whence they sprung!

WATSON:
—There's nothing to tell. They come, they go, they suck. Case closed, no pattern to be found.

HOLMES:
There is always a pattern. If one looks closely enough.

WATSON:
Also, it's private!

HOLMES:
And nothing is truly private. Not to me.

WATSON:
Yikes.

Holmes grabs a piece of paper

HOLMES:
Watson!—look! Ow, ow, ow—a paper cut! A paper cut!

WATSON:
(very disinterested, still busily cleaning) Ouchie.

HOLMES:
(waving the finger around, evocatively, trying to get Watson's attention) Feeling woozy, Watson?!! Don't you want to throw up, don'tyouwanna faint?

WATSON:
—you're not even bleeding.

HOLMES:
—I didn't really cut myself, you know. A small fiction—a control. Is it the blood that triggers you?

WATSON:

Stoppit. I'm not some experiment, and I am not your problem to solve!

HOLMES:

Everything is mine to—

WATSON:

Whatever, whatever! I know how you did that deductive mumbo-jumbo to impress Mrs. Hudson, by the way! Pretending to figure me out, based on like, the hem of my pants or whatever. You cheated!

HOMES:

Me?!!!

WATSON:

You Googled me!

HOLMES:

What?

WATSON:

You knew Mrs. Hudson was bringing around a tenant, and you did some deep-dive to freak me out, God knows why, you could have relied on the apartment full of bones and poisons and probably rodents—but instead, you Googled me and had your fun with your silly little parlor trick. Ha ha ha, very creepy and clever, but I am on to your game.

HOLMES:

No, Watson—I am asking—what is a Google?

WATSON:

What *(is)*... It's a—a page, on the—you type in the bar—and—like—I don't know—little Ask Jeevey gnomes go find you facts. Greatest search engine in human history? *(Watson pulls out her iPhone)* Any of this ring a bell?

HOLMES:

I don't Do The Internet.

WATSON:

...Not even TikToks?!

HOLMES:

I can't afford the mental clutter.

WATSON:

Yes—you seem very concerned with clutter. *(gesturing at the apartment)* So—you really have no desire to connect, withthe wider world of the world-widening-web, like...at all?

HOLMES:
What "Connection" could I wish for the the corrosive mediocrity of the masses?

WATSON:
Again—yikes.

HOLMES:
Let me use a computer analogy, Watson, since you are so obsessed. My brain—is a finely tuned microchip, such as you carry around in your—pocket device.

WATSON:
—you mean my *phone?*

HOLMES:
Right. Your satellite-linked spy tablet. Your wireless—communicator box.

WATSON:
Do you not have—a *cell phone??*

HOLMES:
What I *have* is a comprehensive classical education; intimate understanding of criminal networks; proficiency in hand-to-hand combat arts; plus mastery of the seven pressure point combinations that cause instantaneous death—

WATSON:
Wait, what?

HOLMES:
Paired with an unparalleled attention to detail and ability to formulate complex theories based on the same. Such top-level machine functioning requires a highly-efficient microchip! Now if I were to take—

She grabs Watson's iPhone—

WATSON:
Hey—

HOLMES:
Said highly-specialized microchip, and clutter it with—

Holmes dumps out a nearby very dead plant, and begins sprinkling dirt on the phone

WATSON:
Stop!

HOLMES:
Pollutants—in the form of say, "TikToks"

21

Holmes dumps out the whole potful of dirt onto the phone

WATSON:

Sherlock!

HOLMES:

—The machine could break down entirely! I brook no distractions outside of my focus. I rely on no externals, no technologies, no opinions from the crowd! I stand alone, independent and pure—a finely-crafted tool to my work!

WATSON:

—you're a tool, all right.

Watson picks her phone out of the dirt.

—I still say you're cheating somehow.

HOLMES:

Then I shall have to prove my skills anew! Hark, Watson—a footstep upon the stair! The plot thickens!

WATSON:

What the frig kind of Victorian phraseology is that?

HOLMES:

Somebody's coming! Somebody's coming! Occupy yourself!

WATSON:

Why?!!

HOLMES:

Looking busy is looking important—which allows me to significantly raise my freelance rates! Don't just stand there, woman, act like you're on the job!

Holmes shoves her around as:

WATSON:

But I'm not—I don't—stoppit—WHAT JOB DO YOU MEAN!

A polite knock.

LESTRADE:

Hello? Is anybody home? Hullo?

The door opens—and there stands INSPECTOR LESTRADE. Just what you would expect a detective to look like. Holmes looks him up and down—microbeat:

3.

HOLMES:
—Huh.
Cheez it, Watson—it's the fuzz.

LESTRADE:
—Why. Yes. It is. I am looking to speak to a Holmes? A Ms. Shirley Holmes?

HOLMES:
There is no Shirley. Not now, not ever. But there is *(pointing to herself)* a Sherlock.

LESTRADE:
—What kind of a name is Sherlock?

HOLMES:
It's Greek for "and why exactly, are you here, Officer."

LESTRADE:
Ms. Holmes—I am Inspector Lestrade. I was referred to you by Detective Gregson, whom you worked with on The Case of The Devil's Foot.

WATSON:
Again, those all sound fake.

LESTRADE:
Gregson recently retired, and I am—

HOLMES:
—newly assigned to his post by Scotland Yard.

LESTRADE:
Why—yes. How did you know?

HOLMES:
Elementary. First—your uniform. It's crisp, right off the rack. Your haircut: regulation, within the centimeter, you must have seen the barber yesterday! Your shoes are shining, unsullied, unbroken—you'll soon get a blister upon the left heel. Eager. Detail-oriented. Freshly-costumed. Lestrade, you simply scream: ambition.

LESTRADE:
My God, Ms. Holmes! I could listen to you go on forever!

WATSON:
Careful what you wish for.

HOLMES:
Inspector Lestrade, Dr. Joan Watson.

WATSON:
(as they shake hands) Nope, nope, nope. I am not a Doctor! Not any kind of doctor at all.

LESTRADE:
Pleasure to meet you, Mrs. Watson.

WATSON:
And definitely not a Misses.

LESTRADE:
Oh. *(he holds on to her hand; Watson stares at him)* Hello.

HOLMES:
Why exactly are you here, Lestrade? I assume it is not exclusively to pick up divorcees.

LESTRADE:
Yes. That is no. Not—*(he tries to recover himself)* Hahm. Gregson claimed you're invaluable as an expert on cracking—unusual cases, Ms. Holmes. A sort of—female, latter-day Encyclopedia Brown.

HOLMES:
—Encyclopedia—How DARE you compare me to that—underaged sneaker-sporting hack! I am a deductive consultant without peer, man!!! I take secrets and make solutions!!! *(She kicks something)* Encyclopedia Brown.

LESTRADE:
Alright—/ I say /

HOLMES:
Screw him, him and Sally Kimball too!

LESTRADE:
I'm very sor*ry*!

HOLMES:
They know what they did! *(she kicks more things—bang bang bang bang)*

LESTRADE:
(as Holmes bangs around) Uhhm—anyhow, Ms. Holmes—we've had a—perplexing case open up in the last 36 hours—and—and I should love to see exactly what you are made of.

HOLMES:
(Holmes suddenly whirls and stops kicking) Prepare—to be—astounded. *(Holmes grabs a coat.)* So, Watson?

WATSON:
Sooo, what?

HOLMES:
To the scene of the crime!

WATSON:
What?!!! No, I'm not a cop!

HOLMES:
Pfft, neither am I. Come—the best way to tackle this panic attack issue is by real-world experimentation, under the selective influence of relevant stressors!

WATSON:
What does that mean?

HOLMES:
<u>Don't you wish to be—useful?</u> *(Watson stares at her)*

LESTRADE:
Uh, Holmes—I really—don't think it's appropriate—to have a civilian on the scene.

HOLMES:
Civilian? Watson's no civilian. Can't you tell by her battle-hardened stare?

LESTRADE:
—Thought she just might be depressive.

WATSON:
Thanks.

HOLMES:
I will not take the case without her, Lestrade! She is my medical liaison!

WATSON:
I am not.

HOLMES:
She is my assistant.

WATSON:
No!

HOLMES:
She is... my... roommate!

LESTRADE:
> Uhhhhm, I really don't think that qualifies her to—

But Holmes is already bounding out the door

HOLMES:
> Not a moment to delay!

LESTRADE:
> But you don't even know where we are going!

HOLMES:
> —OH DON'T I?!!!
> To arms, Watson, to arms—the game—is afoot!

4.

The electric buzz of a sign with a letter missing: **OTEL**. *An intensely seedy hotel room—in the corner is a bathtub with the shower curtain drawn. The carpet squishes. Flies buzz. This setting—like all other scenes—can just be delineated. It may all take place in some variation of Apt. 2B.*

HOLMES:
Me first, ME FIRST, OUT OF THE WAY!

Holmes barges through and darts from place to place—looking at the ground, the walls, a seedy, cheap coverlet. She's fast.

LESTRADE:
Aside from forensics, no one has entered since the maid discovered the scene this morning. As you see, Holmes, it's/

HOLMES:
Lestrade—Shush!

LESTRADE:
"Shush"?

HOLMES:
Don't pollute my process, man! Let me survey my canvas!

Holmes begins a very energized inspection, as:

WATSON:
Bluccch. What is this "'otel"? *(to Lestrade)* You said a maid came in here this morning?—is that the mystery?

Holmes is trotting around, muttering to herself. Watson and Lestrade stand together.

LESTRADE:
Yes—not quite the Ritz, is it? I shouldn't sit upon the bed.

WATSON:
Are you kidding? I hope that big dark stain is, just like, soda.

27

HOLMES:
(trotting by, not even looking up) It's not.

WATSON:
Ugghh. That is *disgusting*.

> *Lestrade strides over to the tub—*

LESTRADE:
It is, yes. But I am afraid—that this particular room—has seen—much worse.

> *He pulls the curtain—and the light turns RED for a moment. There, arm hanging limply out of the tub, is a body. Blood streaks the side of the tub. Perhaps the corpse's face, too, is streaked with blood. This body is probably the actress who plays Irene, in a large padded suit, with a hat. Maybe even a mustache. It need not be very convincing.*

WATSON:
AAAAAHHHHHHHHHHHHHHHHHHHHHHH!

> *The light turns back to its normal color.*

HOLMES:
(examining the body, without touching) Fascinating.

> *Watson hides her face.*

LESTRADE:
Are you all right, Watson?

HOLMES:
(staring at Watson) Yes—are you?

WATSON:
(trying not to hyperventilate) Uhhh—that man—is he—is he—

HOLMES:
Oh, he is quite, quite dead. *(she pulls up the body's arm; it drops, evocatively)* Yes.

> *Watson slowly recovers.*

WATSON:
I'm—I'm all right.

HOLMES:
No nausea—chest pains—faintness?

LESTRADE:
You're a doctor—who can't handle death?

WATSON:
I'm not a doctor! But I did—go to medical school. I've seen cadavers, but not—like *that*.

HOLMES:

"There is a scarlet thread of chaos shot through the skein of life, and our duty is to unravel every inch of it."

Watson shivers with a BLEEhhhhh sound

—Who, exactly, is our friend, Lestrade—and how did he come to this pass?

LESTRADE:

Still an open question. We're pulling security tapes from the front desk—

HOLMES:

Cheating!

LESTRADE:

We are running toxicology—

HOLMES:

Double-cheating—

LESTRADE:

And we took fingerprints as well.

HOLMES:

Aaaand the trifecta!

LESTRADE:

I beg your pardon!

HOLMES:

You rely overmuch on externals, Lestrade! Dependence on technology—surveillance tapes this, blood tests that—will make your original thinking flabby and weak and trite! All you need is this— *(she pulls out a magnifying glass)* and a highly-efficient microchip! *(she taps her head)*

LESTRADE:

Microchip?

WATSON:

Don't—don't. She'll mess up your phone.

HOLMES:

What have you actually observed, with your own two feeble and fallible eyes?

LESTRADE:

—The victim seems to have rented the room under a false name, unless we are really mourning the loss of a Mr. I. P. Freely.

HOLMES:

Alas poor Freely.

LESTRADE:
No ID—but his wallet was full of cash. Small change, mostly fives—and some punch-cards from local holes-in-the-wall.

> *Holmes starts rifling through the wallet, tossing cards on the ground; Lestrade tries to catch them*

HOLMES:
Falafel. Kebabs. Chip shops.

> *Lestrade pulls out a red card—waves it at her, significantly.*

LESTRADE:
Plus a card from something called the Free Worker's Union. Take special note of that, Holmes!

HOLMES:
(with considerable condescension) Mhm*m*. Yes, Lestrade. It is *red*. I *see*.

LESTRADE:
He may have dropped the ID somewhere—though theft is possible—as we cannot find his phone. But petty crime aside, we know this man was alone when he died.

HOLMES:
Why do you say that?

LESTRADE:
He checked in by himself. No strange cars in the lot. *(Lestrade tracks the prints:)* And only one set of footprints into the room. It rained last night, and he's tracked mud to the bed. You see the impression in the carpet!

HOLMES:
Look at you, *observing thi*ngs. *(again with the condescending tone:)* That is *very* very good.

LESTRADE:
(goes over his head) Gosh, thanks!—so. Fellow shows up at a seedy hotel—checks in under an assumed name—slashes his wrists. Should be a straightforward case, but—THEN:

> *Lestrade pulls the curtain fully—and there—a big wash of light and sting of sound: DUN DUN DUN! On the wall, behind the corpse, is the word RACHE—written all in blood.*

LESTRADE:
This is why we've brought you in.

HOLMES:
"Rache."

> *Holmes examines the writing.*

WATSON:
What does *(trying out different pronunciations; Holmes corrects her)* "Rache" mean?

LESTRADE:
Well, we've Googled the word—

HOLMES:
Aha! A Google! Yes! I know what that is!

LESTRADE:
—uh-huh. And Rache is—*(checking notes)* "a hunting dog bred in the Middle Ages."

HOLMES:
Well, that's helpful. Good job, the Googles.

LESTRADE:
But it's also German—for *"revenge."* I have a hunch, Holmes—that this "Rache"—may be the key to unlock the entire mystery. I have also Googled—

HOLMES:
Yesyes, very good, excellent, can't waittohear. Watson, give a hand?

Holmes climbs into the tub with the corpse.

WATSON:
Me?

HOLMES:
No, your little brother John in Oklahoma.

WATSON:
/How did you—

HOLMES:
/Yes, YOU Jump on in, the water's fine.

Watson also clambers into the tub with the corpse. She's behind its head, awkwardly. All three of them in there is a tight fit.

WATSON:
Eugwh.

LESTRADE:
AS I was saying, I also Googled—

HOLMES:
LESTRADE ENOUGH WITH THE GOOGLESING! An artist needs space to focus!!!

LESTRADE:
/But—

31

HOLMES:
/Don't "but" me, man, don't "but" me at all! Watson, lift up that arm! *(Watson, wincing lifts up the body's arm.)*

LESTRADE:
(hopefully)—Holmes—isn't there anything at all—that I can do?

HOLMES:
You—can dust the sill for prints.

LESTRADE:
Do you think someone might have come in through the window???

HOLMES:
Sure, buddy. Why not. Really dust it good. *(Lestrade wanders off.)* Watson—look at these incisions.

WATSON:
No, please—I might get sick.

HOLMES:
Yes. You might. Let us experiment.

Watson examines the body's wrists.

WATSON:
Oh—um. There isn't—much gore at all.

HOLMES:
Interesting, isn't that. Little bleeding. But yet—

WATSON:
Yikes.

HOLMES:
Ragged cuts, nasty—really hacked away.

WATSON:
That's a clue?

HOLMES:
—derrrr. And the conclusion is... obviously—

WATSON:
The conclusion is—the conclusion, indeed.

HOLMES:
"Yikes." Let's try an even easier one. Look at this arm, Watson. From this, surely you can tell me the man's profession!

WATSON:
He was a man—who worked. A working man.

HOLMES:
(rolling her eyes) I'll give you a hint. Freckles on the right side of the arm, only.

WATSON:
He was—a dermatologist?

HOLMES:
My God, Watson, how do you get your pants on of a morning?!

WATSON:
OKAY. I give. What does that mean?!!

HOLMES:
Freckles. On the right. Come on, Watson, you can <u>*doooo*</u> it, you can figure i*t ouuuut.*

WATSON:
Hey. Nuh-uh. Do not use that tone with me, okay? I am not Lestrade.

Lestrade is still dusting—

LESTRADE:
HOLMES I THINK I FOUND A—oh no.—That's a bug. *(he fights the bug)* EeeEEEeee!

Lestrade is very afraid the BUG IS ON HIM, THE BUG IS ON HIM, OH GOD WHERE IS IT, OH GOD HAS IT GONE DOWN HIS PANTS?!!

HOLMES:
—Freckles mean prolonged sun exposure—but only on the right side—as one gets in a driver's seat.

WATSON:
Wrong side, SuperBrain. That would be the left.

HOLMES:
Oh you poor benighted American sod. Not in this civilized country.

WATSON:
Wait, Holmes—look here. The nails! The blue-ish tint. He must have had heart trouble.

HOLMES:
Mm! Yes—not that it got him in the end. Alas Poor Freely.

She looks at Watson, considering. Lestrade has wandered back over.

LESTRADE:
So, Sherlock—about this *(Lestrade waves around the red card)* "Free Worker's Union." They're actually a group—of German extraction!—originally named *(very guttural and harsh)* Freie Arbeiterinnen—und Arbeiter-Unions!

WATSON:
Ah, *Deutsche.* The language of love.

HOLMES:

(*to Watson*) Lift his leg.

> *Watson lifts the body's leg. As the two woman clamber around the tub:*

LESTRADE:

What's more, a British branch of this "union" has been organizing in these parts!

HOLMES:

—now the other.

> *Watson lifts the other leg; in order to do so, she has to slide somewhat under the corpse.*

LESTRADE:

Riling up local blue-collar workers! And not only are they committed *class warriors*—they, I'm afraid... are **anarchists**.

HOLMES:

Fascinating.

LESTRADE:

Isn't it?!!!!

HOLMES:

Sorry, Lestrade, what were you saying? I was looking at shoes.

WATSON:

Holmes?—a little help?

> *She is now completely seated under the corpse, as if they are bobsledding.*

LESTRADE:

.... Foreign radicals, Holmes! Anti-government fanatics! This unfortunate fellow must have gotten mixed up with (*gothic horror*) **socialism.**

WATSON:

Wait, are they socialists or anarchists?

LESTRADE:

Whatever! We're talking stone-cold-post-cold-war commies!

> *Holmes clambers out of the tub.*

HOLMES:

Exemplary police work, Lestrade. Primo academy thinking. Now, if you shall pardon me—

> *Holmes jogs towards the exit—Watson is trapped in bobsled mode with the body—*

LESTRADE:

Holmes—are you—going out?

HOLMES:
Yup!

LESTRADE:
Are you planning to tell us where?

HOLMES:
Nope!

WATSON:
SHERLOCK! ARE YOU SERIOUSLY LEAVING ME RIGHT NOW?!!

HOLMES:
And don't you try to follow, Watson! You shall ruin your surprise!

Holmes runs out the front door. Beat.

LESTRADE:
—So, you two are friends?

WATSON:
No. No. Nonononope. We are NOT. And you know how you can tell? Because friends don't leave friends PINNED UNDER STRANGE CORPSES IN BATHTUBS!

LESTRADE:
So you're just "roommates"—then.

Watson tries to wriggle out from under the body

And by that you mean... you are "roommates."

WATSON:
(still trapped)—Boy howdy, Lestrade. You are some detective.

Holmes bounces back in:

HOLMES:
Aaaand I'm back!

WATSON:
Oh good, hope you enjoyed your lil' stroll, CAN YOU PLEASE HELP ME OUT OF THE FREEZING COLD MURDER BUCKET!

Holmes helps Watson out of the tub:

HOLMES:
Anyhow, Lestrade—you were speaking of...

LESTRADE:
Anarchists!

HOLMES:
Right, right, red menace, go on.

LESTRADE:
> These mad Marxist manipulators may have driven this poor fellow to commit suicide—and leave this dread portent behind!!!

HOLMES:
> Just one teensy problem with your Tom Clancy plotline there, Lestrade: this man did not commit suicide, at all.

LESTRADE:
> What?

HOLMES:
> Even Watson could have told you that.

WATSON:
> Uh. *Chyeah. (faking it)* Duh.

LESTRADE:
> Then why is there only one set of footprints into the room?

HOLMES:
> Ah—but note how deeply that set is embedded into the carpet. Our friend in the tub weighs 15 stone. To leave these kind of impressions— you would need a significant addition in weight. *(Lestrade peers at the foot prints)*
> The victim's name—by the way—is Joseph Timothy Drebber.

WATSON:
> Okay, how can you POSSIBLY know THAT?

HOLMES:
> Elementary, my dear Watson.
> Lestrade—you said that no strange cars were seen in the lot! But you neglected to observe that most overlooked of city vehicles—the cockroach of transportation: the unremarkable taxi. There is one parked across the street; Mr. Drebber is the driver!
>> *Holmes quickly lifts and drops the corpse's limbs as she rockets through, then rifles through the wallet—bounces to the door, as:*
>
> Freckled arm from decades of driving. Wear on the shoe, back of the heel—habitual stopping and starting. Wallet full of punch cards from stand-and-eat food spots, with small bills for change from fare. And no need to carry an ID, when it's posted in his vehicle! When I ran out of here—I simply looked in the taxi's window. His cabbie's license is in the back seat: picture and all.

LESTRADE:
> So—what—this cabbie Drebber walks from his taxi—staggering under the weight—of his own murderer?

HOLMES:
His *passenger...* in more ways than one.

LESTRADE:
What kind of a cab driver carries a charge in from the rain?

HOLMES:
The one who's expecting a rather generous tip. Maybe "just the tip, just for a second." He carried her right to the bed.

LESTRADE:
Her?

HOLMES:
Here—*(she points to the floor)*—one small divot. A stiletto.
And what's—more—*(she carefully lifts one hair from the coverlet)*—she is a red-head.

LESTRADE:
Egads!

HOLMES:
—the sheets are not disturbed; no consummation. But look at the compression—*(points at the carpet)* here. He was dragged over to the tub, before his wrists were cut—clothes-on.

LESTRADE:
Astounding, Holmes! Pure artistry!

HOLMES:
Obviously.

LESTRADE:
But—it still doesn't explain—this. *(pointing to "Rache")* Scotland Yard is—most interested in "Rache"!

HOLMES:
I imagine that was the intent.

LESTRADE:
—Do you mean—because it's some kind of a MESSAGE? Left—from this man's MURDERER?

WATSON:
Wait—WAIT—*(faking a British accent)* BY JOVE, I'VE GOT IT!

HOLMES:
Have you.

WATSON:
Rache—we've been thinking it's German. But maybe it's the beginning of Rach—EL.

37

LESTRADE:
Rachel!

WATSON:
Rachel is the name of the killer!

LESTRADE:
RACHEL THE RED-HEADED ANARCHIST!

WATSON:
But wait—if it's "Rachel", it's not an anarchist at all, because then it's not German—

LESTRADE:
But if it's not anarchist assassins, then what was the card doing in his wallet—

WATSON:
Well maybe that's a coincidence!

LESTRADE:
Well maybe the name Rachel is a coincidence!!!

WATSON:
Well maybe *you're* a coincidence!!!!!

LESTRADE:
Well what does that even—

> *Lestrade's cell phone ring tone goes off, noisily; Lestrade's ring tone is something absolutely ridiculous. Maybe it's "Bad Boys." Maybe it's "Put on A Happy Face." Maybe it's "Milkshake." These are all non-proscriptive suggestions - you can go with whatever silly pop earworm song you like. The song just must be something recognizable - a popular but absurd song - a song that you absolutely cannot take seriously, however hard you try, especially given that it's coming from a grown man's phone.[1]*

LESTRADE:
This isn't over. *(into his phone:)* Lestrade!

> *He walks away, listening to the phone:*

WATSON:
Holmes, I think we've cracked it!

HOLMES:
Mm, yes, I saw your playdate. You'd be licking paste off each other's fingers, next.

> *Holmes watches Lestrade, who is pacing*

Interesting—that Drebber's phone was missing, isn't it.

---

[1] See note regarding Music Usage in the play's front matter.

WATSON:

Nah. I mean, whatever. The red-haired maybe-anarchist assassin must have taken it! Whatever her name is. Even though it's totally Rachel!!!

Holmes goes back to the body

HOLMES:

Nice gold wedding ring here. She didn't take that.

Holmes screws the ring off the body's finger

Watson—look under his ring. Notice anything?

WATSON:

—a finger? *(Holmes pfffts)* Wait—a finger... with no tan line.

Lestrade closes the curtain around the tub—Holmes keeps the ring—as:

LESTRADE:

Holmes—you have done it again.

They've found the red-haired woman.

5.

As we begin, the scene transitions around Holmes & Watson into a much nicer second hotel room—this time, the sign says HOTEL, with the H. The new hotel room is denoted by white drop cloths laid over all the furniture. Watson is excited.

WATSON:
Oh my God, so is her name Rachel?!!! And is she German? And is she a communist?!!!

HOLMES:
Anarchist.

WATSON:
Whatever!!! Oh my GodohmyGod, I'm so—weirdly excited!—oo, this is a much nicer hotel! Wait, did the anarchists pay for it? Is Rachel really a Black Widow-like agent of some neo-international class assassin ring?? HOW FAR UP—DOES THIS THING GO?!!!

HOLMES:
Watson. You're babbling.

WATSON:
(nigh-giggling, then:)—wait, should I even be here? If you're going to, like, *(crime-fighting:)* bust down doors and make arrests?!!

HOLMES:
—there's not going to be an arrest.

Holmes is pulling on a rain poncho.

WATSON:
What/ do you—

HOLMES:
You may want to put this on.

WATSON:
A rain coat? *(even as she pulls it on)* Okay, um, why would I need a—
Two GIANT buckets of blood are thrown on Holmes & Watson. Just— blood splashed everywhere.

WATSON:

AhhHHHHhhHHHHHHHHHHHHHH!!!!!!

LESTRADE:

Welcome to Scene 5, ladies. Sorry it's a bit—messy.

WATSON:

AaaaaAAAAaaah!

LESTRADE:

Yes, this one is—not a suicide.

HOLMES:

Lestrade, you're *learning*.

WATSON:

This is—this is—oh my God, is that an EYE?!!

HOLMES:

About three-quarters of one.

WATSON:

Nnnghhh there is blood everywhere—on the walls, on the ceiling—

LESTRADE:

Under the stove. And I wouldn't recommend looking into the box safe, that's where the killer put the victim's—*(his phone rings—that stupid ring tone song again)* Hang on.

He steps away.

WATSON:

Put the whaaaat? *(a la* Se7en*)* What's in the box? What's in the boxxxx?

HOLMES:

—Feeling woozy, Watson?

WATSON:

Feeling VERY DISTURBED, THANK you!

HOLMES:

But not having a panic attack!

WATSON:

(with some surprise) No. No, I guess—not. *(beat; Watson wipes some blood off; she is almost happy)* Well! Huh!

HOLMES:

Don't sit there, Watson, unless you like spleen.

WATSON:

(jumping up) BLEGH.

And all of this—is really the work—of the red-haired woman?

HOLMES:
No. All of this—is what is left—of the red-haired woman.

Lestrade re-enters—he holds up the phone, in confirmation with info:

LESTRADE:
Checked in under a fake name—but the clerk recognized her. She's in regularly, with men, as a—professional companion. A lady of the night. A member of Mrs. Warren's profes—

HOLMES:
She was a sex worker. You can say it, Lestrade, we're not 14.

LESTRADE:
I just didn't like to, in front of Watson.

WATSON:
...uh?

LESTRADE:
It is clear what happened here, of course!

HOLMES:
Is it?

LESTRADE:
(proudly) Elementary, my dear Holmes. *(he and Watson may attempt a high five; if so, they miss)* The anarchists only gain in brutality with each crime! This woman—this *professional*, was involved in a kind of a post-Soviet honeypot operation to ensnare Mr. Drebber. It went wrong—and they did this as a sign—to other members of the—the Communists Consortium: Protect the Party—or Pay the Price!

HOLMES:
By Jove, Lestrade. You're so close. It's shocking how close you are.

LESTRADE:
Really?!!!

HOLMES:
No.

LESTRADE:
Oh, and I suppose you know exactly who these Marxist murderers are???

HOLMES:
Yes. Obviously. Aaaaand—*(They look expectantly at her—she takes a breath—and then bounces up to leave, cheerfully)*

LESTRADE:
Aaaaand??

HOLMES:

And so we ought to go! Nothing left to learn!

WATSON:

We're just—leaving?

LESTRADE:

(hysterical) MY GOD, WOMAN, A HORDE OF VICIOUS PINKO ASSASSINS IS ON THE LOOSE!

HOLMES:

Lestrade, in this morning's *Guardian*, I leaked a story that Mr. Drebber's wedding ring was stolen from the scene of the first crime. When they call for comment, note that a gold men's ring, size 10, has now been found. *(she holds up the ring)*

LESTRADE:

Did—you—steal evidence from my crime scene, Holmes? That is *very* very illeg/al—

HOLMES:

In your follow-up to the press, say that if the public has information on said ring, they should contact 221 Baker Street, Number 2B.

LESTRADE:

—and then what?!!

HOLMES:

And then... *(looking around the blood-covered room)* then we should order a pizza.

6.

Lestrade and Watson clean up the blood-covered... everything as the scene transitions back to dingy #2B and Holmes orders the pizza from her landline—yes!—on the wall.

HOLMES:
Yes, I'd like—double cheese, pepperoni, sausage—extra marinara on the side. *(observing the blood clean-up)* Lots and lots of marinara.

WATSON:
Uch.

HOLMES:
What, Watson?

WATSON:
It's not like, normal, you know—*(she picks up a particularly bloody bit)*—running right from a horrific crime-scene to cavalierly ordering a pizza while calmly waiting for an unknown number of assassins to ring the front bell.

HOLMES:
It's not "normal," no.

WATSON:
I mean I guess you seem to be, like, having fun.

HOLMES:
Why, yes, Watson. I am. Aren't you?

Watson looks at her; half-smiles—

LESTRADE:
It is queasy-making, Holmes—knowing that any moment, a mad mass of Marxist murderers may muscle in menacingly! How much longer should we be held in suspense?

HOLMES:
Not much longer at all. *(she starts up)* There was a sound—on the stairs.

WATSON:
That's probably the pizza!

HOLMES:
—it is not. Back away from the door, Watson.

WATSON:
Oh my God ohmyGod ohmyGod.

HOLMES:
Keep your wits about you, Lestrade!

A creak on the stairs, as:

WATSON:
OhmyGodohmyGodohmyGod—

HOLMES:
No sudden movements, now—

WATSON:	**LESTRADE:**
OhmiGODOHMYGOD/ OHMYGODOHMYGOD	OHMYGODOHMYGOD

HOLMES:
3—2—and *(she WHIPS the door open)*

LESTRADE:
FREEZE, YOU COMMIE SCUM!!!!

Lestrade unexpectedly pulls out a gun at MRS. DREBBER—*late 50s, grey hair, in a housecoat—she freezes, terrified. She has on a wedding ring. She is the least threatening person imaginable—like a sweet aunt who collects doilies. She trembles in fear. They all WHOA and scatter at the sight of the gun.*

MRS. DREBBER:
—don't shoot!!!!!!!

LESTRADE:
HANDS UP, EMMA GOLDMAN!

MRS. DREBBER:
I'm here about the ring!

HOLMES:
Lestrade—

LESTRADE:
I BET YOU ARE, CHAIRMAN MAO!

WATSON:
/Lestrade!

LESTRADE:
NOT ANOTHER STEP, LENIN, OR I'LL BLAST YOU BACK TO SIBERIA !

45

HOLMES:
Lestrade, stop! This is neither Sacco nor Vanzetti! In fact—

MRS. DREBBER:
I am Mrs. Lucy Drebber!

WATSON:
(to Lestrade)—Joseph Drebber's *broken-hearted widow.*

MRS. DREBBER:
What d'you mean, calling me a "commie"?—I voted for Margaret Thatcher!

WATSON:
Why do you even have a gun, Lestrade?! Isn't that not like a British policeman thing?!

LESTRADE:
I got a special dispensation!!! Because of the **socialists.**

as he waves the gun around expressively—they all duck and "ah"

HOLMES:
Lestrade—you just stand by the door.

LESTRADE:
Right! Have no fear, ladies. I'll keep the Watch. The Red Tide—shall not pass!!

Lestrade lives his best superspy life, as:

HOLMES:
Mrs. Drebber, I am Sherlock Holmes, this is Joan Watson—

LESTRADE:
Come and get it, you Soviet scum!

HOLMES:
And that is the cream of London law enforcement.

LESTRADE:
(still in fantasy land, a la commercial:) "Makin' commies cry for their mommies. Lestrade, Thursdays on BBC 1."

HOLMES:
(gesturing for her to sit) You are here, I am sure—about your husband's ring.

MRS. DREBBER:
On the news, they said—it had been stolen, and found? Who could have—taken it? Does you think—Joe didn't commit suicide at all?

HOLMES:
The case is still open.

MRS. DREBBER:
May I—see it? *(starting to get weepy)* It's—it's all I have left of him now!

WATSON:
Oh—

MRS. DREBBER:
School sweethearts, Joe and I were—married, 30-odd years! *(she weeps)*

WATSON:
Mrs. Drebber, I am just, so so—sorry for your lo—

Watson starts to sit next to her

HOLMES:
(With sudden urgency) <u>Watson.</u> Why don't you get her some tea.

Watson moves away

MRS. DREBBER:
(getting worked up) I do beg pardon, my dear, for my—f-f—fuss—I just can't believe—he's truly gone!

She weeps. Watson presses her hand to her own heart.

HOLMES:
Mrs. Drebber—*(Mrs. Drebber sobs)* if you will please just stop your—*(sobs)* noisy—*(sobs)* moisture—making—*(sobs sobs)*

WATSON:
Sherlock!

HOLMES:
I am happy to give you what you are owed. Behold—Mr. Drebber's ring, and you shall get it—*(she produces the ring—Mrs. Drebber reaches for it, but Holmes pulls back, and catches Mrs. Drebber's hand)* If you'll just—let me—SEE!

Holmes and Mrs. Drebber engage in a real wrestling match in a big tumble of waving limbs; or, really, Holmes just sort of waylays her, grabbing her hand violently and taking off her wedding ring. Lestrade and Watson try to rescue Mrs. Drebber. Much hubbub, all of this simultaneously

MRS. DREBBER:	**WATSON:**
—what are you—	HOLMES! WHAT ARE
let go of me—help!	DOING! SHE'S A
HELP!	LITTLE OLD LADY!
	WHAT ARE YOU,
	ROBBING HER!

47

HOLMES:
    LET! ME! SEE!

LESTRADE:
    I say, Holmes—Holmes! We are not allowed to lay hands on the elderly!

Holmes emerges victorious with both rings; Mrs. Drebber is half on the floor

HOLMES:
A-HA-HA!

MRS. DREBBER:
Oh, my bones!!!!

HOLMES:
30 years of marriage, you say!!! And yet your ring—and his ring—do not seem—<u>to match!</u>

LESTRADE:
—My God, Holmes—are you implying that she is an impostor?!

MRS. DREBBER:
I am Lucy Drebber—three decades Joe's wife!

HOLMES:
And your ring, Mrs. Drebber, is tarnished and dull, as one might expect after such a long-standing partnership! But Mr. Drebber's—is shining. As if it had been *wiped clean!*

    she holds up the ring

I had this ring examined closely by forensics. Technology, these days! They can sniff out even the slightest trace of evidence—and they found a fingerprint—smudged upon the inside of Joe Drebber's ring. Can you guess—whose?

    Beat.

MRS. DREBBER:
I must have touched his hand—a dozen times, every day!

HOLMES:
Ah—but—this—particular fingerprint—was smudged in blood.

WATSON:
—But what about the red-headed anarchist?!!

HOLMES:
Here is your red-headed red-herring—caught red-handed.
LESTRADE, THE DOOR!

    Mrs. Drebber darts towards the door, VERY fast—Lestrade raises his pistol.

Mrs. Drebber—sit—and tell us when you'd finally—had enough.

Beat.

MRS. DREBBER:
Decades and decades I gave that man. Years of cooking his breakfast, ironing his shirts, making his bed—all just so. Joe wanted his wife kept at home! I cut myself off from the world for the love of him—but I always thought that he could see—all that I had given up.

As Mrs. Drebber tells the story, we see it acted out, very like a film noir, or a soap opera—sexy, melodramatic. Lestrade stands in for Mr. Drebber.

HOLMES:
—did you find red hairs?

MRS. DREBBER:
I found the texts he sent to her, that—red-headed *professional*: prices, negotiations—acts. He didn't even try to hide the phone; thought I would never catch on! He was so sure—there were no surprises left in me!

HOLMES:
But there were.

Mrs. Drebber and Lestrade act this all out—she pretends to put on a wig, make herself up—

MRS. DREBBER:
I dressed myself to the nines. Threw on a red wig—knew he'd like that, didn't I—colored contacts, loads of makeup—called his dispatch for a ride. I feared he'd recognize me right off. But he never did—not when I got in the cab—not when I started flirting with him! Not even when I suggested a hotel! He knew right where to go! How many women—had he taken there?!

Again, Lestrade and Mrs. Drebber enact this:

It was raining, and he carried me into the room—like a—bridegroom bringing me across the threshold! He laid me on the bed, I looked him straight in the eye, kept thinking any moment now, surely after all these years... it's me—it's ME, JOE—**SEE ME, SEE ME!!!!!** But all he ever saw was what he wanted.
He unzipped his fly. I whipped off the wig!

The dream Joe Drebber staggers and falls

It was his heart, Inspector Holmes! His heart—was never good!

HOLMES:
And then?

MRS. DREBBER:
—I panicked! Did you ever see *The Sopranos*, when they chop up the—but it's not so easy, in real life. I made such a mess—I had to make it look like self-harm!

She hacks and hacks and hacks—the light turns red.

HOLMES:
You destroyed his phone, to get rid of the texts. Shoved his ring back upon his finger; he had taken it off?

The fantasy fades as...

MRS. DREBBER:
You can see why I was angry. But I just—wanted to scare him, Inspector! Show him—who I really was!

HOLMES:
As you showed the other woman?
I said the fingerprint on the ring was smudged in blood.
I did not say—whose.
She died first—didn't she, Mrs. Drebber?

MRS. DREBBER:
(*something very, very dangerous is here:*) Red-headed tart had it coming.

*She **giggles**. Beat, then back:*

I just don't know—how I left my fingerprint, I was so careful to wipe it clean!

HOLMES:
Oh, there were never any fingerprints on this ring.

She tosses it to Mrs. Drebber, who catches it in shock

Let alone in the first victim's blood.

MRS. DREBBER:
What?!! But—but you can't mislead a suspect into confession—

HOLMES:
Sure I can! I'm not the po-lice!

MRS. DREBBER:
What.

HOLMES:
I'm a deductive consultant!

MRS. DREBBER:
WHAT?!!!

HOLMES:
(*cheerfully*) I lied! Well, I hypothesized—which is almost ly—

MRS. DREBBER:

(panting—Watson starts towards her, but Holmes stops Watson) Oh, God, oh God, what have I done? Oh—oh no!!!!!

Mrs. Drebber suddenly passes out, limp.

HOLMES:

Lestrade—no closer. She'll go for the pistol. *(Lestrade stops)*

LESTRADE:

She really seems to be out cold.

HOLMES:

Underestimation is a dangerous habit, Inspector. Just ask Joe Drebber.

conversationally, to Mrs. Drebber's still body

Mrs. Drebber—you claimed your husband was already dead, when you dragged him to the tub. But the shock didn't quite finish him off, did it? His heart was indeed weak—he didn't bleed much. But he was still alive.

Was he conscious—when you cut into his wrists?

Mrs. Drebber's eyes pop open. Both Lestrade and Watson jump.

MRS. DREBBER:

Got his attention then, didn't I? *(she **giggles**)*

LESTRADE:

Alright, Mrs. Up now, slowly.

He begins to get Mrs. Drebber out.

HOLMES:

I do have one question. How did you come up with the misdirection of "Rache"? It was clever to send us on the wrong path—completely took in lesser minds—

WATSON:

Thanks, Holmes—

HOLMES:

—Did you find the Free Workers Union card, and improvise?

MRS. DREBBER:

There are places on the web, Ms. Holmes—where one may find creative solutions for certain urgent problems.

*She leans in—and **nigh-hisses:***

You're not the only one with clever ideas.

*She **giggles**. Holmes looks after her as she's led away—as the giggles turn into mad, unfettered laughter, bigger and bigger and bigger—*

7.

The next day. Apt 2B. Holmes lounges on the dingy sofa, playing with the finger bone. Watson plugs away at a laptop. Lestrade is hanging between them, with a six-pack of beer.

LESTRADE:
A toast to you, Holmes; an oddball, arguably; a robot, potentially;—a genius, for certain!

HOLMES:
It was—satisfactory, to encounter a minor challenge, again. Pity it was solved so quickly.

LESTRADE:
(joking) Well—here's to many more murders to come, ey?

Lestrade offers a beer to Holmes:

HOLMES:
Not my substance of choice.

LESTRADE:
Watson?

WATSON:
Uh—okay. Thanks. Should you be drinking on duty?

LESTRADE:
I'm a naughty boy at heart. *(He winks at Watson, who is tip-tapping away at her keyboard.)*

WATSON:
Hey, would you describe Mrs. Drebber as: "mousy"? I mean, you know, before she turned out to be. A psycho killer.

HOLMES:
Qu'est que c'est. Are you writing about our exploits, Watson?

WATSON:
Tweeting about 'em! @JoanWatson's 20-part thread on the #StudyinScarlet. True crime is big now. Goin' a wee bit viral with hashtag murder hashtag revenge hashtag Rache!

HOLMES:
>I have no idea what you just said.
>>*she slams Watson's laptop shut; Watson "awks"*
>But I know I don't like it.

LESTRADE:
>Holmes—how *did* you know—not to chase after "Rache"?

HOLMES:
>Sorry, Lestrade. That is between me... and my book of casework.
>>*Holmes reaches beneath the sofa—and pulls out a very large, thick book. It has a hard cover. Maybe it is also covered with big fourth grader diary-style stickers that say things like KEEP OUT and PRIVATE. Maybe there are glittery unicorns. Maybe Garfield stickers. The more fourth grade the better.*

LESTRADE:
>Harriet the Spy, are you?

HOLMES:
>That snot-nosed amateur! She owes me thirty-two dollars.

WATSON:
>[what]

HOLMES:
>This book—contains a detailed overview of every villain in London: their connections, histories, social circles. In it, I have compiled enough sensitive information to make or sink an entire criminal empire... not to mention build a sizable fortune.

LESTRADE:
>Love to take a peek in those pages, Holmes.

HOLMES:
>Over my dead body.

LESTRADE:
>Well, maybe some day.

HOLMES:
>I will tell you one thing—I fear there was a deeper force at work in this case.

LESTRADE:
>What do you mean?

HOLMES:
>There's a greater brain behind this than Mrs. Drebber. Something—some*one*—is afoot. And there is no answer to whom—even in my pages.

Holmes sits on her book, shielding it from Lestrade—then begins rolling a joint.

WATSON:

(re: the weed) Holmes!!!! *(pointing at Lestrade)* Ther fehrz *(the fuzz)*!

HOLMES:

He's "drinking on duty"!

LESTRADE:

I should be off anyhow. Ladies—try not to get into trouble. Especially you, Watz.

He smiles at Watson, who is taken aback—exits, humming the 90s hip-hop song. Watson waves the smoke away.

WATSON:

Sherlock—it's noon.

HOLMES:

It helps to dull the compulsion—the nagging, painful urge.

WATSON:

What "urge."

HOLMES:

(holding in a big toke) The urge—to deduct. *(she lets it out)*

WATSON:

Holmes—not to beg for punishment—but how *did* you know not to be fooled by the anarchism stuff?

HOLMES:

—You see this puzzle, Watson?

Holmes pulls out a large puzzle box from beneath the coffee table—pictured on the front of it, are two fuzzy, doe-eyed kittens—the puzzle's picture.

WATSON:

D'awww. Where'd you get DAT?

HOLMES:

(defensively) Quarantine was long. I got desperate.

WATSON:

Aww, wook at the baby kitties.

HOLMES:

Right, fine, whatever—

WATSON:

Wook at their wittew wiskews!

54

HOLMES:

—this puzzle—how would you piece it together?

WATSON:

Um, I'd find the kittens' eyes, first, sort those out. Then I'd find their itty baby fuzzy toesies, and then their teeny weeny tailsies ohmyGoddeiw sweet smushy noses! *(puppeting the box)* Mewmewmewmew!

HOLMES:

WATSON, FOCUS.

Watson waves the smoke away from her.

WATSON:

Sorry, that stuff is strong.

HOLMES:

You make the same mistake as many amateurs—focusing only on what you wish the final picture to be, and not accepting the pieces as they come.

Holmes dumps the pieces of the puzzle all over the coffee table as Watson, paying attention but getting a little stoned—gets a bag of Doritos and busts into them as Holmes talks—

HOLMES:

But if you are intent on twisting facts to reach a pre-determined end—you will never be open to seeing alternate truths. To find other ways individual elements fit! You do *this*, deductively speaking!

Holmes begins smacking all the pieces together evocatively—maybe she even grabs a convenient hammer or bone and beats it—

WATSON:

Ack, don't hit the pretty little kitties!!!

Holmes messes the pieces around on the table

HOLMES:

Lestrade was dead-set upon his anarchist fantasy—and so he seemed to miss a whole host of other clues, muscling the facts to suit his theories!

WATSON:

Meow meow meow.

They both unthinkingly eat out of the bag, companionably

HOLMES:

Always take information on its own merit, Watson. Eliminate the impossible, embrace the improbable. But—never—NEVER—jump to kittens.

WATSON:

(surveying the mess)—so I guess I'll be the one cleaning this up.

> *She begins to sweep them up. But Holmes is still, head-cocked—there's a step on the stairs.*

HOLMES:

Watson! Stop! Wipe your fingers!

> *She snatches the bag from Watson and throws it on the floor.*

WATSON:

(horrified) My Doritos!

HOLMES:

/Look busy and important! This is a big one, coming up the stairs!

WATSON:

How do you—

HOLMES:

The same way I know everything, Watson!!!
I Never!!! jump!!! to!!!! kittens!!!!

> *Watson, ineffectively, tries to look busy—she gets cheese dust on everything. Holmes springs to open the door, then acts extremely relaxed as she opens it*

8.

A man stands there in a Donald Trump mask. This is ELLIOT MONK: Texan, start-up mogul, tech billionaire, and sleaze.

HOLMES:
—Cheez it, Watson. It's your former president.

WATSON:
—Not *my* president.

Watson crunches the chips angrily.

MONK:
Pardon my disguise, Ms. Holmes—but I am here on behalf of a high-profile figure, and I—he can't afford to be exposed—any more than I—he already has been.

WATSON
Wow. Subtle, dude.

MONK
Can I—he—we speak in private, ma'am?

HOLMES:
I don't believe in privacy. A prejudice I should think that you would share—Mister Monk.

MONK:
(Monk whips off his mask) Wha—how did you know?!!

HOLMES:
Elementary. Your left wrist.

MONK:
—you mean the freckle?

HOLMES:
Your watch, sir. Platinum face; dual diamond dials; crocodile band—all summing up to a Patek Philippe 480 Chronograph. Worth 3.6 million American dollars—*(Watson "awks")* and only two ever made. Unless you are the 75-year-old patriarch of Dubai's royal family—I am addressing Mr. Elliot Monk, CEO; Austin-based tech wunderkind; and billionaire, many times over.

Next visit, wear a Timex.

MONK:

Wow, Ms. Holmes—just—wow. No secret is safe with you!

HOLMES:

Flattering, coming from one of the top information-peddlers in the world. Mr. Monk made his fortune in social media start-ups, Watson. He lures in the unwary—getting them to sign away personal information to access addictive apps—

WATSON:

Hey—didn't you invent Bling Crash? *(Bling Crash is Watson's absolute favorite app)*

HOLMES:

Then mining their data—

WATSON:

Wait—

HOLMES:

And selling it to the highest bidder.

WATSON:

Is that why I keep getting ads?

HOLMES:

All kinds of unscrupulous parties will pay handsomely for access to people's private information—won't they, Monk?

MONK:

Gotta love the free market!

HOLMES:

Behold, Watson—the price of your "connecting."

MONK:

As you say, Ms. Holmes, I've managed to make a—decent living—in the private sector. *(he taps the watch)* But along the way, I had some mistakes in my personal life. I mean, don't get me wrong—I've dated lots of chicks. Hot chicks. Socialites. Newscasters. Models. Foot models.

> *Watson gags audibly*

But not one of 'em ever could compare to—Irene. *(pronounced like Irenee)*

WATSON:

Irenee? What, like—Irene—but a little extra?

MONK:

Ms. Irene Adler. And as extra as they come.

Irene's had a varied career—lots of different skills—but nowadays—she works as a "professional companion". A lady of the night. A member of Mrs. Warren's—

WATSON:
We GET it.

MONK:
I saw her, in that capacity, for about a year. And during that time—we made a—certain—tape.

HOLMES:
Of course you did—

MONK:
And she kept the only copy.

HOLMES:
Of course she would—

MONK:
And now she's threatening to release it.

HOLMES:
Of course she is.

MONK:
I want to become a better man, Ms. Holmes! Leave the past in the past! But Irene refuses to let me move on!

WATSON:
I mean—there's a lot of risqué footage out in the world, nowadays. How exposed could this tape really leave you?

MONK:
Very exposed. *(beat)* Very very very exposed.

WATSON:
Yeah, I'm gonna need more details. Could you—just draw me a picture—no wait, show me on the skeleton—

MONK:
I'm willing to spend a LOT to get this film out of her hands. Whatever your normal rate, I'll double it. Triple it. Quadruple it.

HOLMES:
This is not my kind of case, Mr. Monk. Why don't you hire some inferior sleuth?

MONK:
Oh, I've hired men to follow her, hack her computer, break into her place—

WATSON:
Wow, okay, Prince Charming—

MONK:
But every one of 'em failed. They say—the only person who could ever match Irene, Holmes—is you.

WATSON:
Hellooo, didn't you hear her the first time? You're not her type of client, buddy. B-bye! *(she starts pushing him out)*

MONK:
Just because I'm not a hero, lady, doesn't make Irene the heroine!

WATSON:
Adios, Tex! Sorry you're in the queso! Don't let the door hit you in the ten-gallons on the way out! *(she pushes him most the way out)*

MONK:
(to Holmes) Name your price—and I'll meet it!

WATSON:
Maybe she doesn't HAVE one! *(she gets him most of the way out; he sticks his foot in the door)*

MONK:
We all do, in the end. Holmes, Holmes, baby—call m—

Watson slams the door in his face.

WATSON:
Well. May I just say—G-BLEGH.

HOLMES:
Mr. Monk certainly wins no prizes for charm.

WATSON:
Oh he's a true-blue Yankee Doodle Scumbag, ain't he? And did you notice—the ring? *(she holds up her left hand like The Finger)*

HOLMES:
I did, yes. *(Watson snorts and starts cleaning)* But isn't there something—irresistible, Watson, about a problem—that no one else can solve?

WATSON:
NO!

HOLMES:
I'm not jumping to kittens. There just may be merit in taking on this case!

WATSON:
Even with the sleaziness and the skeeziness and his business summing up to everything you hate?!

HOLMES:
I don't "hate" anyone, Watson, or anything.
Such feelings are immaterial. Clutter, clutter, clutter.

WATSON:
Well, I've never wanted to mug a dude more in my life. A 3.6 Million dollar watch! I'd like to hold him down, and punch and punch, till all the money flew out of him like a piñata—just pow! Pow! Pow! Pow pow pow!

IRENE:
So you understand my position.

> *Watson jumps a mile. Behind her, has appeared—IRENE ADLER. Adler is striking. Stunning. Dressed to the nines, like a steampunk dream—and on her, it's CHIC. Powerfully charm. And in this moment—totally in control.*

WATSON:
Ahh!
Holmes, I thought you could hear anybody who was coming up the stairs!

HOLMES:
(really taken aback) So—did—I. *(she stares at Irene)* Ms.—Irene Adler, I presume?

> *Irene flops comfortably on the couch.*

IRENE:
—Ms. Sherlock Holmes. Hello, gorgeous.

> *Irene grins. Black out.*

INTERMISSION.

ACT TWO

1.

Moriarty may position Irene Adler as the actors reset—smiles at the audience—he disappears—and we whirl right back into:

HOLMES:
Ms. Irene Adler, I presume?

IRENE:
Ms. Sherlock Holmes. Hello, gorgeous.

Holmes just stares at her—Irene twists and gives that killer grin to Watson.

And Joan Watson, the Not-A-Doctor.
Ladies—I've heard so much about you.

WATSON:
Um—from whom?

Irene, shrugging and grinning, picks a random piece of detritus off a table.

IRENE:
"Nice" place you have here, gals. A real Laverne-and-Shirley-Go-To-Hell Aesthetic.

HOLMES:
Thank you, Ms. Adler.

WATSON:
What, no!—no "thank you."

Irene and Sherlock are staring at each other.

IRENE:
You're so welcome, Ms. Holmes—and you may call me Irene.

WATSON:
Listen, "Irene", you have a lot of chutzpah coming in here and making snarky comments! We can't afford an interior designer, okay? We don't make our money the hard way.

IRENE:
That's true—for me, it is always hard.

WATSON:
Ew.—you are—vulgar.

IRENE:
Men like it. Women too. Do you like it, Sherlock?

HOLMES:
I don't—know.

WATSON:
—*(pure dread)* Oh noooo.

Irene waggles her fingers back and forth at the two roommates.

IRENE:
What exactly is this dynamic, ladies?

WATSON:
Wha'dyou mean?

IRENE:
What's your deal?

WATSON:
What?

HOLMES:
Watson—is my assistant.

WATSON:
Not—I'm not. Holmes is my—

HOLMES:
Mentor.

WATSON:
No—she's not! She is my—

HOLMES:
Roommate. We are roommates.

WATSON:
Yeah!

IRENE:
You needn't be embarrassed to have a mentor, Watson. I had one, once upon a time. She is much-missed. *(Irene smiles at Holmes, who looks at her.)*

WATSON:
Holmes is not my mentor!!! And—whatever, whatever. I am nobody's assistant, I went to medical school, FYI, and graduated first in my class!!!

IRENE:
    And NOW—you are the... Not-A-Doctor. My, those student loans must sting.

    Holmes sits near Irene on the sofa, gingerly; she stares as if Adler is a strange and beautiful alien.

HOLMES:
    Ms. Adler—may I...

IRENE:
    You, Sherlock—may do anything you like.

HOLMES:
    May I *ask*—How much would it cost Elliot Monk—for you to hand over this—tape?

IRENE:
    Oh, I'm not out for money, honey. I do just fine. No—this is about—something else.
    I regret to inform you ladies, that Elliot's intends to "turn over a new leaf" by launching a campaign to buy himself a powerful Senate seat, back in your good old U. S. of A.

WATSON:
    (appalled) Eoh.

IRENE:
    Mm. What's more, he's rebranding as a *(imitating Monk)* "Champion of Family Values." If he *chooses* to announce his candidacy, I will *choose* to release the footage. Unlike Elliot, I am pro-whatever-choice.

WATSON:
    Exactly what is on this frigging tape???

IRENE:
    Let's just say—I really have him over a barrel. He runs, I run the clips.

HOLMES:
    So—why, exactly, have you come *here*, Ms. Adler?

IRENE:
    To warn you, Sherlock. *(she gets close)* Watch out.
    A bigger game is afoot—and you couldn't sniff out my secrets if you tried.

HOLMES:
    —Trust me, Ms. Adler—if I wanted to—I could.

    They are getting closer and closer

IRENE:
    I think you want to.

HOLMES:
I think you want me to want to.

IRENE:
I think you want me to want you to want me to—

> *They're practically nose to nose.*

WATSON:
What is going ON?

IRENE:
Pipe down, baby. The adults are talking.

WATSON:
Lady—you—are—you—are really—psht.

IRENE:
What a way with words.

WATSON:
You—you—*(classic raspberry:)* PBBTH.

IRENE:
—Devastating.—Well, must run, gals. Cosmos and mani-pedis soon!

> *Irene begins to leave.*

Oh—Holmes—one last thing. Do you happen to know: the work of Sun Tzu?

WATSON:
What?

HOLMES:
By heart. Of course.

WATSON:
Seriously—what?

IRENE:
"Preparation... may lie within our joined hands, *(she comes palm to palm with Holmes)* but defeat of the enemy—is from the enemy himself."

WATSON:
—what the frig?!

HOLMES:
(still joined hands with Irene) It is—*The Art of War,* Watson.

IRENE:
—and what an artist you are, Sherlock.
But you're not the only one with clever ideas.

> *Holmes starts; Irene steps back.*

Ta-ta.

She exits

WATSON:

Well. Monk was right about one thing, Holmes. Just because he's a villain, doesn't make her a heroine. She is—she is—

HOLMES:

—striking.

WATSON:

—okay, that is not what I was going to say at ALL.

HOLMES:

Facial symmetry, vocal tenor—hair lustrousness—that is, objectively, a very attractive human being.

WATSON:

But her *personality*.

HOLMES:

Yes.

WATSON:

I mean, like, if you go for that—obvious—femme-fatale—whatever. Barf. *(Holmes snorts)* And what was with all those random non-sequiturs?!!!! "Watch out!" and "The game's afoot" and "Chicken Soup for the Confucian Soul" or whatever.

HOLMES:

—I'm taking on the case, Watson.

WATSON:

What?!! You're going to help Elliot Monk buy his way into office?!!

HOLMES:

A mystery is a mystery.

WATSON:

So you really do have your price?

HOLMES:

I really do have my reasons.

Holmes has started rummaging through a trunk

Come now, Watson—no sulking—have some faith in your mentor!

WATSON:

YOU ARE NOT MY MENTOR!
Besides—did you ever think that maybe you can't succeed where all those other detectives failed?! Maybe even Sherlock Holmes is fallible! Maybe you won't find the tape!

HOLMES:

Ms. Adler is going to show it to me, herself.

WATSON:

How? Through the devastating pull of your personal charms?

HOLMES:

Don't be ludicrous, Watson. Through the all-consuming power—of disguise.

She tosses Watson a nun's habit.

2.

Outside of Irene's apartment—the street. Holmes and Watson put the nuns' habits on as:

WATSON:
Do you just own these habits?

HOLMES:
(sarcastically) No. I rent them, like a fool.

WATSON:
(she struggles with the headdress) I'm not convinced about this, Holmes.

HOLMES:
You're a very credible nun, Watson! You've got the celibate scowl down pat. Now, let's hear your Irish accent.

WATSON:
/What?

HOLMES:
/Nuns. Catholics. The U.K. Come on, you're not in Topeka anymore! Get into the role!

WATSON:
(making vaguely Irish sounds; she is very bad) "Hi—be—deedly—doo. Kiss the Blarney Stone. They're always after me Lucky Charms!"

HOLMES:
(as Watson experimentally capers around like a leprechaun, singing "Danny Boy") Well. Good thing I'm an expert improviser.

WATSON:
(practicing) "Top O' The Mornin'! Erin Go Bragh! Angela's Ashes!"

HOLMES:
Now, this—is the address of Ms. Adler's flat—

WATSON:
"Patty O'Furniture. Cassie O'Keyboard. Jalapen O'Popper!"

HOLMES:
—and it is almost two o'clock. My operative will soon be in place!

WATSON:

(trying to do the accent still; failing badly) What operative? What is this plan? Are we going to perform an exorcism upon her,... mee wee Shamrock? *(going full pirate)* Arr.

HOLMES:

Hush, Watson. Better for you to be a genuine dupe than an unconvincing liar.

Watson "aAAawks" in her bad dialect.

Now stand right here.

WATSON:

(back to American) Um, why?

HOLMES:

—don't you trust me?

WATSON:

(feeling bad) I—well—Holmes—(I)

HOLMES:

Stand very still—don't move a muscle—and—

Holmes hauls back and smacks Watson across the face.

WATSON:

—OW!

HOLMES:

Take the hit like a woman!

Holmes smacks Watson repeatedly.

WATSON:

OW OW WHY ARE YOU DOING THIS

HOLMES:

This doesn't trigger your panic attack? No faintness, no nausea?!

WATSON:

No, although I am getting royally pissed off—*(Holmes smacks her one last time)* STOPPIT

HOLMES:

Alrighty, let's try another tactic.

Holmes begins hitting herself in the face.

WATSON:

—what are you doing?!!

HOLMES:

An experiment! How does this make you feel?!!!

Holmes slaps herself, over and over. Watson is beginning to sway.

WATSON:
That you're in-sane

Holmes escalates into an orgy of self-hitting:

HOLMES:
And this *(slap)*—and this *(slap)*—and this *(Slap slap slap)*! Ha—HA! *(SLAP)*

WATSON:
—Yi-ikes.

Watson abruptly faints.

HOLMES:
Fascinating. *(She starts hopping around, flapping in her robes, assuming an Irish accent)* Help! Help! Jesus, Mary, and Joseph, will nobody aid two spotless brides of the Lord!

Irene pops her head out of the door.

IRENE:
Hello?

HOLMES:
Miss! Miss! Help! Ruffians came—and tried to rob us—ran that away, the scoundrels, may God forgive their wretched souls!

IRENE:
Oh no! Shall I call the police??

HOLMES:
(wringing her hands) Bless you, my dear, I can't wish the rascals behind bars. As Mother Superior says, Sister Margaret Mary, you've too much softness in your spirit! *(she puppets Watson's unconscious body)* But Sister Mary Margaret has fainted, poor Lamb!

She holds the unconscious Watson up.

IRENE:
Here, this is my flat—let's get her inside.

Irene goes to Watson's feet to haul her inside.

HOLMES:
Oh thank you, you angel, you restore my weary faith in the worth of this wicked world—!

Watson is beginning to regain consciousness:

WATSON:
Oof, where the frig am—

Holmes slaps herself again as Irene's back is turned

Oah ma Gah.

Watson faints again.

HOLMES:
Mary Margaret! Mary Margaret! Don't go towards the light!

Irene and Holmes support Watson inside of—

3.

Irene's flat. A sofa—and above it—a framed portrait or photograph of Irene, preferably classic and beautiful; maybe even in 19th century portraiture style. Very simple, but classy.

HOLMES:
Just sling her down anywhere.
>*They dump Watson like a sack of potatoes.*

IRENE:
And are *you* all right, Sister—

HOLMES:
Sister Margaret Mary.

IRENE:
Mary Margaret and Margaret Mary?

HOLMES:
—Catholics.

IRENE:
It looks like you took quite a beating, yourself.
>*Irene feels Holmes for injuries. She is <u>very</u> thorough. Holmes jerks, evocatively.*

HOLMES:
Oo. Umm. That *(starting to panic)*—oo—tickles!

IRENE:
Don't squirm, sister. I am told—that I have very sweet little hands.
>*She holds Holmes' face. She is very close.*

HOLMES:
(clearing her throat) Could—I—trouble you for a cup of water?`

IRENE:
Of course! You poor sainted angel. *(crossing herself)* You're just too pure for this sinful plane.
>*Irene exits, smiling. Holmes immediately starts investigating the room.*

WATSON:

(*regaining consciousness*) Holmes? Did you—slap me?

HOLMES:

Don't be absurd. You must have low blood sugar, Watson—now lie down before she comes back!!

WATSON:

We're in her apartment?!! She actually bought it?!!

HOLMES:

Of course she did, I'm the Meryl Streep of nun impersonators. No seams in the walls, nor safes—but don't worry, the clock has just hit two.

WATSON:

What happens at—

A big big BOOM; the room nigh rocks—and smoke starts blowing in.

WATSON:

Sherlock, what the frig?!! Did you blow up her frigging car?!!

HOLMES:

Of course not. I simply hired a boy to set a bomb amongst her trash bins, and also

BOY'S VOICE (O.S.):

FIRE FIRE!

HOLMES:

Raise an alarm.

BOY'S VOICE (O.S.):

FIRE FIRE FIRE!

WATSON:

You set a BOMB?

HOLMES:

A *smoke* bomb, Watson, don't be so dramatic.—HELP HELP ALL THE FLAMES OF HELL SHALL ENGULF US! FIRE! FIRE! DEATH AND DESTRUCTION! HELP!

Smoke is really pouring in; Irene runs in.

IRENE:

/What in the—

HOLMES:

/MY GOD, WOMAN, YOUR HOUSE IS AFLAME—SAVE YOUR CHILDREN AND YOUR PETS—(*she clutches on to Watson, even as she notes that Irene has gone to the picture frame, and put a hand to it*) Sister Mary Margaret! Sister Mary Margaret! Rouse yourself, the Devil has come for your sins at last!!!

Irene looks out the window—

IRENE:

—It's not a fire—it's some kid in my bins. Hey, you!

Holmes begins to "wheeze"

HOLMES:

Oh, this terrible smoke. Oh, my asthma—I hear Heaven calling me home!

Irene puts the picture frame back into place.

IRENE:

Let's get you out of here. Mary Margaret—can you walk?

WATSON:

(trying and miserably failing to do Irish) Faith—an begorrahh, oi don't roightly know, moi pretty—

Holmes jumps to cover her mouth

HOLMES:

—she's under a vow of silence! But if you will only help her out—the Lord shall guide my steps!

IRENE:

(supporting Watson out) Come, sister.

WATSON:

(dropping the Irish accent altogether) AhhhHHhhHH that tickles

As Irene supports Watson outside, Holmes, still preaching, goes over to the picture frame—feels around, swings it open—and behind it—she finds a bright pink USB. As she does, she keeps yelling offstage:

HOLMES:

Oh, Miss—bless you—you'll be rewarded in the life to come! I see a nimbus of light all 'round your head! I can hear—the celestial—choirs—now!

She slips the USB into her pocket—closes the frame.
As she does:

Hallelujah! Hallelujah. Hallelujah....

A rock version of Handel's Messiah plays as we transition into:

4.

Holmes, Watson, and Lestrade lounge around the dingy flat. Holmes is horizontal on the couch, depressed, talking to the pillow.

HOLMES:
Ho, hum, hum, ho, all is flat and insipid, there is no originality in misdoing anymore.

LESTRADE:
I don't see why you're sulking, Holmes. Anyone would think you'd failed.

HOLMES:
Well, hardly one for the Book, is it? *(she pulls out her book, moodily)* It's no Case of the Dancing Men or Adventure of the Golden Monkey.

WATSON:
Again—all sound fake.

HOLMES:
Alas, this particular case—is not worth memorializing. *(she throws the book from her, moodily; Lestrade eyes it, even as—)*

LESTRADE:
Well, I think it was rather clever of you. Nuns, and smoke bombs, and all that!

WATSON:
I'm sorry, why is Lestrade here again?

HOLMES:
I need an audience who appreciates my genius.

LESTRADE:
Besides, Watz—you know you love my company. *(he winks at her)* How did you plan it out, Holmes?

HOLMES:
To discover what a person treasures, threaten its security. The moment Ms. Adler thought fire might destroy her copy of the tape—she moved to secure it, much as a mother might instinctively

try to save her child. A bit disappointing—I thought Irene was something—special.

LESTRADE:
But you've gotten the big payday from Monk!

HOLMES:
Yes—like so many great artists, I sullied my vision for filthy lucre.

Holmes twirls the pink USB on its little lanyard.

And this BCE—

WATSON
USB

HOLMES
ASD

WATSON
USB

HOLMES AND WATSON
USB

HOLMES
is my soulless reward.

LESTRADE:
You didn't give the tape to Monk?

HOLMES:
I haven't sold out that far. It'll stay in safe hands.

WATSON:
Speaking of Monk—Twitter says he's announcing any minute.

The door bell ding-dongs

HOLMES:
(deeply depressed) Get the door, Watson.

Watson clicks on the TV with a remote—as she goes to the door, one eye on the TV—one on Twitter—

WATSON:
Guess we should watch the funeral.

She switches on the TV and "The Star Spangled Banner" plays on the channel, as a pizza girl arrives at the door—her hat pulled down to obscure her face. Watson is still mostly concentrating on the TV.

WATSON:
Pizza is here, Holmes?

HOLMES:
I'm too disillusioned to eat.

PIZZA GIRL:
>It's pre-paid, Miss.

WATSON:
>Oh, thanks, Lestrade! Can you—

>*Watson tosses Lestrade the remote—*

LESTRADE:
>What channel?

WATSON:
>—here's a fiver.

>*Watson pulls out a note, and hands it to the pizza girl, who tips her hat.*

PIZZA GIRL:
>Have a good evening—Ms. Sherlock Holmes.

HOLMES:
>*(looks up)* Watson—

WATSON:
>Shh-sh-shsh! It's on.

>*The TV blares. We need not see it, only hear it.*

MONK (V.O.):
>It's time to leave the past where it belongs—embrace the future. And that's why I'm announcin' my candidacy for Senator of the Great State of Texas—where I'll stand for old fashioned values, morality—and Warm American Pie. *(he chuckles)* Yum yum yum yum.

>*The sound of applause and cheering.*

REPORTER (V.O.):
>Mr. Monk—Mr. Monk—first question:

MONK:
>Yessir?—

REPORTER (V.O.):
>In light of this new campaign—would you care to comment on the tape now circulating on social media?

MONK (V.O.):
>The—what?

REPORTER (V.O.):
>Yes, sir. The one released just moments ago.

MONK (V.O.):
>*(he may be about to cry)* The... tape?

LESTRADE:
>The tape?

WATSON:
The tape?!!

HOLMES:
The... tape!!!

> *They all jump for the USB at once with BIG YELLS, but Holmes gets there first. Watson pulls out her phone.*

REPORTER (V.O.):
Due to the EXTREMELY explicit nature of this footage, we advise parental discretion in—

WATSON:
The clip is on Twitter. Monk is getting tagged in it, over and over—it's going viral!

> *Lestrade looks over her shoulder.*

LESTRADE:
Oh.

WATSON:
Oh, my.

LESTRADE:
I think you're looking at it upside down, Watson.

WATSON:
I am when it's done right.

> *Lestrade and Watson both watch the video, wincing—heads close, bobbing slightly—as:*

HOLMES:
Watson—did you order a pizza?

WATSON:
(Still looking at the screen:) Me? No. Lestrade got it for us!

LESTRADE:
—No I didn't.

> *They all look up—as Holmes flips open the pizza box. On the inside of the lid, is written:*

HOLMES:
"Dear Holmes and mentee—"

WATSON:
Oh come ON.

HOLMES:
"Haven't laughed that much at nuns since *Sister Act 2*. Thought you might learn from the classics, Sherlock—
P.S.—you're cute."

WATSON:
I can't believe I tipped her!

Holmes strides over to Watson's laptop—puts in the USB:

HOLMES:
"You're—cute?"

LESTRADE:
So if that was—and she was—and this isn't—then what is on the USB?

Holmes presses a button—and music fills the air: "O Dolce Mani" from Tosca.

HOLMES:
O Dolce Mani! "Sweet little hands"—Don't you understand, Watson?!

WATSON:
Um, no?

HOLMES:
It's from *Tosca*. Act three—Mario, led to his mock-execution!

WATSON:
That's all Greek to me, Sherlock.

HOLMES:
No, no—Italian! You hear?

Italians are singing—Holmes sways with the music, joyful, playing air violin—hands in the air:

HOLMES:
"Ecco un artista!"
What an artist!!!!

The Tosca *plays as the scene transitions—*

5.

Moriarty appears again.

MORIARTY:
And so, Irene Adler escapes to extort another day! But Mr. Monk's filthy lucre is still good. And so Sherlock can afford to take on more and more fascinating cases!

> *The women start running in place, as if in montage. The music is very Batman-and-Robin-on-a-caper.*

MORIARTY:
Win! Win! Win! Mystery after mystery solved! Headline after headline plastered! It's a bonanza of criminal absurdity for our intrepid gal-pals!
The Case of the Speckled Band!

> *A bunch of cheesy rubber snakes is thrown at them—they keep running—*

WATSON:
Snakes! Why did it have to be snakes!

MORIARTY:
The Adventure of the Blue Goose!

> *A big bunch of feathers is thrown on the two women—with much honking*

HOLMES:
Geese! Why did it have to be geese!

MORIARTY:
The Infamous Hound of the Baskervilles!

> *An unearthly howl sounds—the women are still running—*

WATSON:
Wait, Holmes—we're not going to even stop for that?!!

HOLMES:
Keep going!

WATSON:
But it's the most famous one, people will expect it!

HOLMES:
We can't afford a giant spectral dog, Watson!!!
This is a small-cast show with a post-pandemic budget!!! Keep running!

MORIARTY:
But they could NOT outrun—a growing sense of danger!
In interrogation, in confession—they heard the same refrain from criminals:

ALL:
"You're not the only one with clever ideas."

The women stop, suddenly.

MORIARTY:
But what could it mean? There are no answers to be found!

HOLMES:
Not. Yet.

MORIARTY:
Even Sherlock Holmes can fail...

Moriarty smiles and melts away. Holmes paces.

HOLMES:
It's driving me MAD, Watson! Time after time, criminals are coming up with solutions—far beyond their ken. There's something—someone—behind it all. If there's a me, doesn't it follow there's a counter-me, out there—taunting, testing. Why?!!!

WATSON:
You sound like you should be raving on Facebook about perverts in pizza parlors.

HOLMES:
I have no idea what you just said. There's a pattern, there's always a pattern—a meaning—somewhere. I've only—got to find it, and I'll discover my match! Eliminate the impossible, embrace the improbable—but never jump to kittens—

Watson and Lestrade stand on the street outside of Baker Street.
Watson is eating Doritos, messily.

WATSON:
She's obsessed with the idea that there's some evil force behind it all. A single mastermind, maybe, or, like, some criminal consortium. And it makes her insufferable to live with! She's up at all hours—playing air violin at top volume—smoking everything but the houseplants! The other day I caught her running electrodes into our toilet!

LESTRADE:
(as Watson grunts and shakes the chip bag right into her mouth) Watson—what's your deal?

WATSON:
My "deal"? *(Watson wipes chip dust from her mouth.)*

LESTRADE:
You are—divorced, yes?

WATSON:
Yeah.

LESTRADE:
From a man?

WATSON:
Yeah.

LESTRADE:
So I'm a man too.

WATSON:
—Yeah?

LESTRADE:
And I've got a weakness for mouthy American girls covered in artificial cheese dust. When can I buy you a beer?

WATSON:
—Lestrade. I have—trust issues.

LESTRADE:
—are you and Sherlock a thing?

WATSON:
No. Why does everybody ask that?

LESTRADE:
You seem very attached to her.

WATSON:
I have issues, period.

LESTRADE:
You two are just friends, then.

WATSON:
Sherlock doesn't have "friends."

LESTRADE:
Is she—yknow—into girls?

WATSON:
I don't think she's into humans.

LESTRADE:
Ha!

WATSON:
—seriously. We're all just facts and figures to her, problems to be solved by that hyper-efficient robot brain. Boop boop boop boop bleep!

LESTRADE:
Well, she certainly seemed to like Irene Adler.

WATSON:
Irene is just—just—that was a million cases ago, and I'm sure Holmes doesn't even think about her anymore, and neither do I—the slinky, smarmy, slippery little—whatever!

She throws the empty bag of Doritos, angrily.

LESTRADE:
Spoken like a truly disinterested party. I'm sure she cares about you, Watson.

WATSON:
You SAY that. But we've worked together on all of these cases now—and I just feel like—every time I think I earn her regard or her like, camaraderie, or even basic respect—she goes and she runs electrodes. Into. My toilet.

LESTRADE:
No wonder you have trust issues. C'mon, Watz, grab a pint with me. Holmes & Watson,—of course you're always placing second. Watson & Lestrade—I'll let you come first.

WATSON:
... wow.

LESTRADE:
—Think about it.

He reaches into his pocket—hands her a small bag of Doritos. She takes them—he tips his hat and walks away—Watson takes out her keys to enter the door, when she's waylaid by:

MRS. HUDSON:
Oh, Doctor Watson! Doctor Watson!

WATSON:
Not Doctor, Mrs. Hudson—

MRS. HUDSON:
Whatever, whatever—thank God you're home! I've been so worried about Shirley!

WATSON:
Shir?—Oh, you mean Sherlock.

MRS. HUDSON:
What kind of a name is—

WATSON:
It's Italian for "this joke is getting old." What exactly is the problem?

MRS. HUDSON:
A few hours ago, I heard some terrible thumps coming from upstairs—I called out repeatedly to Ms. Holmes, but she never answered!

WATSON:
I wouldn't worry—you know she's been moody lately.

MRS. HUDSON:
It's been quiet upstairs—almost TOO quiet. *(significantly, with great fear)* And—Ms. Watson—she has not played a note of her music *all morning!*

WATSON:
—Huh!

MRS. HUDSON:
She's not always done well when alone, you know—despite all her talk. And she's been rabbiting on about some awful super-villain enemy she's made—and I am very frightened to think—what dangerous murderous types may be creeping up to my very doorstep!

Watson begins letting herself into 2B—

WATSON:
Holmes is just over-indulging her considerable imagination, Mrs. Hudson. I assure you that you were never in any material danger, and neither is Sherlock, and really, there is no need to be so melodram—

She opens the door—and there, splayed across the floor at a terrible angle—is the prone body of Sherlock Holmes.

MRS. HUDSON:
EAAAGGGHHHHHHHHHHHH!!!

Watson runs to Holmes' side. She feels for a pulse—rather professionally—

WATSON:
Holmes! Mrs. Hudson—call 9-1-1!

MRS. HUDSON:
Call wot?!! Oh SHIRLEY! SHIRLEY YOU'VE BEEN MURDERED!

WATSON:
She's still breathing!—call 9-1-1!

MRS. HUDSON:
I DON'T KNOW WHAT THAT IS

WATSON:
Emergency services—paramedics! What number do you use in this country?

Holmes' head pops up.

HOLMES:
9-9-9

WATSON:
Thank you, yes, call *(9)*—Holmes!

Holmes sits up, completely unharmed.

HOLMES:
No panic attack, Watson? No weakness or nausea?

WATSON:
I'm so glad you're alive, Sherlock—because now I get to kill you.

Mrs. Hudson sags.

MRS. HUDSON:
OoOoO, it was just—a—another, oh and you are—oo I feel faint.

WATSON:
Ugh—okay, now I do, too.

Watson sways. Holmes observes.

HOLMES:
Watson, head between your knees. Mrs. Hudson—"put on a happy face"—for you've no one to blame but your self.

MRS. HUDSON:
Wot?!

HOLMES:
If I've told you once, I've told you a million—to start anticipating my surprises. *(she pounces at her, jokingly)* EN GARDE!

MRS. HUDSON:
I—I—SHIRLEY, I AM RAISING YOUR RENT!

She exits—slamming the door, in high dudgeon; then just as they open their mouths to speak, she re-opens the door suddenly, scaring the bejesus out of them

FRIG IT!!! *(slams it again)*

WATSON:
Well.—I hope that you are happy.

HOLMES:
I am, actually! It was a very effective experiment!

WATSON:
STOP RUNNING TESTS ON PEOPLE, DOCTOR FRANKENSTEIN, THIS IS NOT THAT PARTICULAR NOVEL!

HOLMES:
Don't you find it interesting, Watson, that you were not incapacitated by my seemingly-mortal injury—in fact, that you sprang to action?

WATSON:
No.

HOLMES:
Isn't it fascinating that moments later, Mrs. Hudson's genuine distress made you feel ill?

WATSON:
Nope.

HOLMES:
It does not impel you to more deeply plumb your inner depths? To explore and unpack this conundrum?!!

WATSON:
Not even a little bit.

HOLMES:
Well, aren't you a sour old cow.

WATSON:
It's a waste of your time, Holmes, to tackle this particular puzzle. Trust me, I have tried, again and again. There's no fixing it.

HOLMES:
Maybe you're drawing the wrong conclusions, or observing unpertinent facts. Maybe you're jumping to kittens.

WATSON:
The friggity fragging kittens! IF I give you some backstory, WILL you finally quit it.

HOLMES:
—It is painful, Watson, to have an unresolved mystery—humming, discordant, in my ear.

Beat.

WATSON:
Listen—it just—quit working.

HOLMES:
What did?

WATSON:
Me. My brain. I had too much—clutter.

> *Watson never cries at all, during the entire story; she is as removed as she can manage*

You'd never guess, but your slightly directionless, social-media-addicted "sidekick"... was once considered one of the most promising young doctors in America.

HOLMES:
I did in fact guess. But continue.

WATSON:
Type A—overachiever, all my life. Best student in my class throughout college—and then, right into med school, Ivy League—again, always number one. Right on to residency at one of the best hospitals in New York, working in the E.R, where I met a celebrated surgeon, whom I eventually married in a big splashy wedding—whole page in the Vows Column! Ran five miles every morning, drank eight glasses of water every day, and journaled every night!

HOLMES:
Sounds terrible.

WATSON:
No—it was—the exact life I—manifested. Exciting work. Big house in Yonkers. Kids on the horizon. Everything going to plan—and then, yknow. 2020.

HOLMES:
Ah.

WATSON:
My husband, he was never great with patients. Surgeons need to be dispassionate, rather than compassionate. But I was—was always hands-on, took the time to chat, got to know people. I had—bedside manner.
But when it was happening—
You were wrapped in layers and layers of PPE. They duct-taped six feet from the beds, where they guessed you might be safe. The E.R. was overflowing, patients crowded in the hallways. There was no time to hold people's hands. And I just saw... whatever. I saw a lot. But hey, I survived!

HOLMES:
Indeed.

87

WATSON:
> I expected, you know—when everything would settle down, then I'd get back to normal too, pop right back into my previous life. But of course, it didn't really stop, did it.
> One night, a kid came in to the E.R. Minor wound; he had cut his hand on a knife. We were relieved—on the floor, to have a normal case. I walked in, with my chart, took one look at this kid's bleeding hand—the tears in his eyes, and—boom. Laid out flat.

HOLMES:
> You fainted.

WATSON:
> —After that—every day I went into work.—whole panic attack smorgasbord. Chest pains, nausea, faintness, difficulty breathing.
> Everyone was very nice at first; patient. But eventually: what use is a doctor who can't—.
> I lost my job, the house in Yonkers. Even lost the husband—as I said—he wasn't so good at compassion.
> It didn't stop. But <u>I did</u>.
> And here I am.
> So see—no more mystery; it's not part of some bigger meaning. Sometimes life—just sucks, and there is no solution.

HOLMES:
> There is always a solution.

WATSON:
> There are no kittens here, Sherlock.

HOLMES:
> And there are always kittens.

WATSON:
> Right.
> You're gonna leave me alone about it, though, yeah? Now that I've given you this big confession? Sherlock? *(Holmes has perked up, listening, and suddenly walked away from her)* Holmes, I want you to swear—

HOLMES:
> Shhhh!!!! Outside—that step—I know it!

WATSON:
> —of course.

HOLMES:
> *(frantically shoving her around)* Look busy look busy the busiest you've ever looked!!!!

WATSON:
Do we have to go through this whole rigamorale every *(time)*—
HOLMES:
Watson—it's her!
WATSON:
Her who? Her wh*(o)*—oh no.
HOLMES:
But she is—*(she's listening to something)*—she is *(listening)* ... Irene!

6.

> *Holmes whips open the door just in time to catch Irene, who half-falls in, battered and bruised and bleeding. It is very romantic, really. Watson instantly feels faint.*

IRENE:
Hello Sherlock. How's tricks?

WATSON:
Oh my God—blech. Ugggh. *(she goes weak at the knees)*

HOLMES:
Ms. Adler—you are hurt.

IRENE:
Ever the great detective.

> *Holmes examines her, gently*

HOLMES:
Shall I get you an icepack?

IRENE:
Pack, no. Ice, yes. Put it in some whiskey.

WATSON:
Blergh.

> *Watson moans, head between her knees*

IRENE:
I'm the one who got beaten up, Watson, I don't know why you're moaning.

WATSON
Werg.

> *Holmes puts the ice pack on Adler's face; Irene holds on to it, staring into her eyes.*

IRENE
Mmmmm.Sherlock. That does feel nice.

> *Holmes steps back.*

HOLMES:
And—what else may I—do for you today.

IRENE:
While I have a long list of suggestions, darling—I'm here in a purely professional capacity.

WATSON:
(still with her head between her knees) We don't need your services, Irene!!!

IRENE:
As if you could afford them. No, Sherlock—*(to Holmes)* I want to hire you. You see—*(she grabs Holmes' hand—suddenly very serious)*—he won't take no for an answer.

HOLMES:
He—who?

IRENE:
They call him... Moriarty.

> *Holmes gently extricates her hand*

HOLMES:
I've never heard the name.

IRENE:
You wouldn't have. Nobody's ever met the man. He's invisible—shapeless, formless. But they say he sees—everything.

WATSON:
(still with her head between her knees) What, like Santa Claus?

IRENE:
Read the room, Watson.
Word on the street is that Moriarty was once a professor of advanced economics—a leader of strategic planning for multinational companies. The foremost mind in his field, until he realized there was a greater fortune to be made—in the deep net.
Moriarty runs the biggest remote marketplace on the dark web, but he doesn't sell goods. He now heads a think tank for the illegal underground—offering creative solutions for criminals in a pickle.

HOLMES:
"You're not the only one with clever ideas."

IRENE:
I got a text last week from an untraceable number. It was Moriarty, with an offer. He wanted me to collect information on clients; sell it back to him—at a commission that even I found shocking. And I am hard to shock.

WATSON:
(still with her head between her knees) I just bet.

IRENE:
But I didn't want to get into bed with a guy like that—

WATSON:
(briefly looks up, then drops back down)—Okay, that one's too easy even for me.

IRENE:
—and he didn't take the rejection well.

> *she winces as she applies the ice pack*

The men who jumped me—were sending a message: I must cooperate—or else.

HOLMES:
A bribe and a threat. The old carrot and stick.

IRENE:
(genuinely shaken up) There's no telling what he can do, Sherlock. Moriarty has fingers in everything: arms trafficking, illegal pornography—international espionage, and on and on and... I need you to get him to reveal himself... before it's too late. Besides, our intentions are aligned on this one, aren't they?

HOLMES:
Are they?

> *Irene gets up, moves towards Sherlock—fluidly.*

IRENE:
Mm. We're vibing on the same frequency, babe—which is why you cannot resist.

WATSON:
Uh, Sherlock—

IRENE:
Pair with me, Holmes. Partner with me. There's nobody that we can't match!

WATSON:
Sherlock—

IRENE:
Help me, Sherlock Holmes-Kenobi, you're my only hope!

WATSON:
HOLMES. Can I—speak to you for a minute?

IRENE:
Go on. I'll pretend not to hear asides.

Watson pulls Holmes aside.

WATSON:
Do I get a vote about taking on this particular client?!

HOLMES:
Why would you?

WATSON:
—don't you care how I feel about it?

HOLMES:
A case is a case.

WATSON:
Right. Beep beep beep bo beep beep.

HOLMES:
Pardon?

WATSON:
(choosing not to pursue that)—Irene, just, she comes in here all, oh, poor me, and eek, I'm such a victim, and hey, this evil super-villain genius you've been imagining, I just happen to be hunting him too, and oo, here's my irresistible Star Wars quote—

HOLMES:
What is a "Star War?"

WATSON:
—And wherever she is proposing to take you, you absolutely should not go!

IRENE:
Me-ow. Oop, sorry, pretending I can't hear.

HOLMES:
Ms. Adler—I do agree with Watson—that you should not lead me anywhere.

IRENE:
Ouchie.

HOLMES:
You said this Moriarty is a threat to your safety. So you should stay out of sight—while I make inquiries.

IRENE:
Don't you want help?

WATSON:
That's why she has me! Now, Irene, hush, shush, sweetheart, let the adults do the—

HOLMES:
No, Watson. *(Watson balks)* Some things I need to do alone.

WATSON:
—since when?

HOLMES:
Since I draw closer than ever before—to meeting my match.
I do not wish Ms. Adler to be alone, and you do not wish her to be with me. Ergo—I will track down clues, while you stay here, with her.

WATSON:
...You mean she and I have to hang out?? No, come ON. How is THAT the best solution?

IRENE:
—Well *I* am on board with your very wise proposition, Sherlock—or any proposition you should give me, at all—

WATSON:
Okay, if she's gonna stay in our space, she can't keep talking like that. It makes me very uncomfortable—

IRENE:
I guess some brittle, plebeian souls have no capacity for the theatrical—

WATSON:
Yeah, again!—

IRENE:
/And never could hope to understand! *(riding right over her) Speaking* of which—Sherlock, darling—did you happen to approve of the *Tosca*?

HOLMES:
I did. Though I must say—I generally prefer more subtle dramas. Like—Hamlet.

> *Again, Holmes and Irene do this sexual / intellectual inching towards each other, circling.*

WATSON:
Hamlet?

IRENE:
Really.

WATSON:
How is *Hamlet* subtle?

> *Irene gets closer and closer to Holmes*

IRENE:
It's all about confession and revelation.

HOLMES:
And transformation.

WATSON:
Doesn't it end with everybody dead?!

HOLMES:
"The spirit I have seen—May be the devil—"

IRENE:
"—And the devil hath power—to assume a pleasing shape"

> *Irene and Holmes are so so close—*

HOLMES:
"And perhaps abuses me to damn me"

IRENE:
"I'll have grounds more relative than this"

> *Holmes and Irene are SO close*

WATSON:
I hate it here.

HOLMES:
"The play is the thing—"

HOLMES AND IRENE:
"—wherein I'll catch the conscience of the king."

> *Irene nigh-shudders, close enough to breathe Sherlock's breath; climactically—*

IRENE:
Oh. Sherlock, Sherlock!—don't you just *love* the *classics!*

7.

Later. Irene lounges on the couch—Watson stands, watching her every move.

IRENE:
Well. What should we do first, Watz—braid hair, gossip, or make prank calls?
(Irene begins to get up.) Shall I paint your nails, bestie?

Watson darts over, lifts a convenient frying pan.

WATSON:
Hey! You are not slithering out of here, Adler!

IRENE:
Planning to cook me breakfast? Cheeky, I haven't said I'm sleeping over.

WATSON:
This—is in case you get any funny ideas.

IRENE:
—what, about flapjacks?

WATSON:
You—are not cute. And I do not want to banter.

Beat.

IRENE:
Poo.
(gesturing at Watson's forehead) You're getting angry elevens, doll. Is all this—scowling judgement—really about my profession?

Watson doesn't answer

It's a trade like any other. And I learned it from the best.

Beat. Watson doesn't answer

You know, people need connection, now more than ever, Watson. Maybe even Holmes. Maybe even y—

WATSON:

(finally breaking) Oh my God, please please spare me the "sex work is work" hooker-with-a-heart-of-gold-as-emotional-laborer-slash-defacto-therapist speech, I get it, that's not the frigging thing, okay! I don't care what you do!

IRENE:

But you may care *who* I do. Is all this just jealousy over dearest Sherlock?

WATSON:

Why do you have to make everything all—ooh, ahh, oozing with sexy feelingsy-touchy sex. Maybe I just don't want to see her get hurt. Maybe we're friends, you ever think of that!

IRENE:

I believe that you're *her* friend. But—these things—can be a bit—one-sided. *(sing-songy)* Someone has an unrequited crush.

WATSON:

I'll show you a crush. Sit down.

IRENE:

(Irene sits, blithely.)—I don't think you even understand Holmes. She and I are playing at a different game. And you're not—are you? Or do you like the classics?

WATSON:

Yes, whatever, so you can quote Hamlet. Me too. "To be, or not to be—that is the mercy that droppeth—to take against—the tide of times" blahblahblah. *(she runs out of steam—)*

> *Irene, bonelessly, gets up from the couch*

IRENE:

Speaking of 2B!—I heard—that sweet Sherlock keeps a journal of her exploits here.

WATSON:

Where did you hear that? And / hey—

IRENE:

A book detailing the ins and outs of all criminal life in London. Valuable—in the right hands! Or the wrong ones!

> *Watson fruitlessly pursues her—Irene carefully observes, makes a feint, and—digs Sherlock's book out from the puzzle box.*

WATSON:

How / did you—!!!

IRENE:
You—sweetpea—are easier to read than Doctor Seuss. Your eyes went to the book's hiding place the moment I mentioned it; no wonder Sherlock finds you so easy to impress!

> *Irene is moving quickly around the room—it's tag—carrying the book. She spanks Watson with it lightly as she passes.*

WATSON:
Give it back/ and—

> *It becomes a real chase around the couch—Irene is easily ahead.*

IRENE:
Hunter and hunted, hunter and hunted, round and round we go. But who chases and who flees, only Irene Adler knows! 2B or not 2B—you don't know what forces you are playing with!

WATSON:
WHY ARE YOU SO FAST

> *They pause, panting—Watson is in considerably worse shape than Irene—she holds out the frying pan, threateningly.*

IRENE:
My mentor taught me—Adler, make sure you always know where the exits are!

WATSON:
Well, then, she taught you badly!—'cause I'm between you and the door!

IRENE:
The exits—and the light switch.

> *Irene grins, flips the switch—everything goes black.*

WATSON:
Oh, frig.

> *BANG! The sound of someone being hit over the head with a frying pan.*

8.

Sounds of trains. The lights blink on—as Watson, handcuffed behind her back, blinks—waking up to Holmes shaking her. Up above them is a high platform; we cannot see over the edge.

HOLMES:
Watson! Watson, wake up!

WATSON:
(groggily) Holmes—Holmes? *(she struggles)*—am I—handcuffed?

HOLMES:
Don't worry. It's not my first time.
Holmes begins to pick the cuffs.

WATSON:
—how/ did you—?

HOLMES:
There was a note—at the flat—"To discover what a person treasures, threaten its security. Come to the old Kenyon Junction Station."

WATSON:
—what is this place?

HOLMES:
(working on the cuffs) Abandoned transit hub. Trains from London still rattle through, just below that platform up there.
Holmes frees Watson from the cuffs—and they are covered with faux fur, as are sold by sex shops. Holmes holds them up.

HOLMES:
Now that *is* a first.

WATSON:
Oh my God—Holmes—she has it!!!

HOLMES:
Who has what?

99

WATSON:
Irene stole your book—your book about the criminal underground! The whole Moriarty thing was just a ruse to get you out of the apartment!!!! I told you not to trust her: she's just—some common criminal!

IRENE:
Not common at all.

Irene steps out—she is holding a pink handgun.

No sudden moves now, gals.

HOLMES:
Ms. Adler. What a surprise.

IRENE:
Sorry to bring you out to the 'burbs, Sherlock. But I needed a nice, neutral space with lots of exits. Plus we're at the end of the line! Seemed apt.

HOLMES:
We knew we might come to this, Irene.

IRENE:
We sure did, babe. But as old Sun Tzu says: "Engage opponents as they expect; while you wait for the extraordinary moment."

WATSON:
WHAT is with you and the SUN TZU, Adler, it is EXHAUSTING.

IRENE:
Quiet, Watson! The adults are talking!

WATSON:
Lady—I will slap you so hard your hair will go back to its natural col—

HOLMES:
(harshly) Watson, hush!

WATSON:
Et tu, Sherlock?

HOLMES:
As Irene said—the game is afoot.

WATSON:
Really?!! So you're officially taking her side now?! *(gesturing wildly at the gun)* I—I don't know what you see in her!!!

HOLMES:
One word, Watson.
Bait.

Just offstage, a ring tone plays: Lestrade's signature dumb ring tone song.

HOLMES:

Irene—I don't believe you know—Police Inspector Lestrade.

Lestrade steps out. He's holding a gun, too; it's black. Watson hops around giddily.

WATSON:

Lestrade?!! LESTRADE! Oh, AMAZING. HAHA HOLMES YOU REALLY ARE A GENIUS. IRENE YOU'RE IN TROUBLE NOW, KIDDO. *(grabbing Lestrade and kissing his face, as:)* LESTRADE, BABY, BUBBELAH, YOU GO AHEAD AND ARREST HER! *(Lestrade calmly turns off his cell ringer as:)*

This woman—this CONwoman—made up a whole scam about the infamous digital super-villain Professor Moriarty, in order to steal from Holmes!!!!!

HOLMES:

No, Watson.

WATSON:

No, wait, Irene IS Professor Moriarty!!!

HOLMES:

No, Watson.

WATSON:

(gasps) No—wait There IS no Moriarty, at all!

LESTRADE:

No, Watson. There is no Lestrade.

WATSON:

—WHAT

LESTRADE / MORIARTY:

Well, there *was* an Inspector Lestrade, once—who was due to transfer into the department at a convenient moment. Now, he's somewhere along the bottom of the Thames.

HOLMES:

—you... are Moriarty.

LESTRADE / MORIARTY:

Underestimation, Holmes—is a dangerous habit.

he turns to Irene

Hello, Irene.

Both Irene and Moriarty swivel and turn their guns upon Holmes & Watson.

WATSON:
–THIS DOES NOT HELP WITH MY TRUST ISSUES.

MORIARTY:
Yes—I'm sorry, darling. I did not find you binge-eating crisps quite as irresistible as I might have claimed. *(he steps towards her; they all react)*

WATSON:
Hey—hey! Back off!

MORIARTY:
Please. It's not you that I want, "Watz." *(Watson "awks")* It's you, Sherlock.

HOLMES:
What?

MORIARTY:
As you've heard, I provide niche services, via the lesser-known channels of the internet: offering ethically-neutral problem-solving to individuals, organizations, and governments.

HOLMES:
"You're not the only one with clever ideas."

MORIARTY:
We are artists working in the same medium, Holmes. I also trade solutions—for secrets.

WATSON:
What the frig does that mean?

MORIARTY:
In dire straits—and straits are so dire nowadays—folks are willing to give access to *extremely* private information, in exchange for easy answers. I collect such sensitive materials—and sell when they accrue maximum value.

WATSON:
You blackmail people?!!

MORIARTY:
Noooo—not just people! Companies, consortiums; countries. I work, as Holmes should be working—on a wider canvas.
I've been so sad for you, Sherlock—watching you waste your talents, locked away in that ratty flat. Hunting down homicidal housewives. Performing P.R. mop-up for perverts. But with the technologies at my disposal—*(Holmes starts drifting towards him)*

WATSON:
Uh, Holmes—?

MORIARTY:

—you could go so much further. Nothing and nobody would be beyond the reach of your skills. Join my network, and there would be no more closed doors, Sherlock. No more
nagging unsolved mysteries. No more *secrets*. *(he reaches out to Holmes)* It's time to connect with your true peer, darling. It's time to—partner.

WATSON:

Holmes—?!

> *he traces one finger down Holmes' face—taps her head*

MORIARTY:

Join your remarkable machine with mine—and we can solve anything... everything.

HOLMES:

Everything.

WATSON:

HOLMES!!!

MORIARTY:

She's gone blue screen, Watson—you're looking at a total reboot.

HOLMES:

Ev-ry... *(Holmes is, indeed, transfixed; still)*

> *Watson snaps her finger, waves her hand in front of Holmes—nothing.*

WATSON:

Sherlock?!!! Hello?!!! HELLO?!!! *(desperately)* WAKE UP!!!

> *Watson shakes her. Holmes is completely frozen.*

MORIARTY:

Irene, drop the gun, you're not helping with the tension.

IRENE:

No thank you. *(she coolly turns the gun towards him)*

MORIARTY:

Now, now—there's no collaboration without trust!

WATSON

So you work for him?!!

IRENE

No.

MORIARTY

Yes.

IRENE:

NO! You said if I brought you Holmes, then you would leave me alone!

MORIARTY:
Oh, Irene with two e's, I'm only asking you to do what you already do, plus a little extra—and you are as extra as they come. You'll be paid accordingly.

IRENE:
I don't work with pimps. But I'll make you a fair trade.
Stay the hell out of my business, Lestra—Moriarty—whomever you are—and you can walk away with this!

She pulls out Holmes' book.

WATSON:
Oh, you—you TOTAL JERK!

IRENE:
Sherlock Holmes' encyclopedic rundown of all the criminal networks in London.

WATSON:
ADLER YOU COMPLETE CREEP!

MORIARTY:
A page-turner, no doubt. But I won't need it, Irene. I already have Sherlock.

IRENE:
She hasn't agreed to work for you!

MORIARTY:
Everybody has their price—and I am exactly who and what Holmes needs.

He reaches out and touches Holmes, possessively.

I—am her match.

Moriarty deftly grabs Watson, and holds the gun to her.

HOLMES:
Hm.

Holmes, delicately, moves away from him

See—that is where you're wrong—Moriarty, Lestrade. Whoever you are.

MORIARTY:
Well. Look who's come back to life—

HOLMES:
I don't need you.

MORIARTY:
Really.

Threateningly swinging the gun from Irene to Watson, and back again.

And which of these lovely ladies is my rival?

HOLMES:

Neither of them. Nobody. I don't need anybody, at all.
Such feelings are immaterial—clutter, clutter, clutter.

MORIARTY:

(testing) Then I suppose you wouldn't mind if I just—

he suddenly grabs Watson and puts the gun to her head; she yells in panic

HOLMES:

What—kill Watson? Sure. Do. Blow her head off. Throw her into the Thames. She has no more secrets to plumb—for I have solved her case.

WATSON:

Sherlock, WHAT THE FRIG?!!!

Holmes has worked her way over to Irene.

HOLMES:

I don't care about Watson, at all, except for the puzzle she presented. Much like Irene—I thought she might be something more, but—nada, niente, bubkis.

IRENE:

Sherlock, honey—that is hurtful.

HOLMES:

I've figured her out, too. And—once the mystery is gone...

Holmes grabs Irene's pink gun—twists it—shoots Irene with her own pistol. Irene drops.

WATSON:

Aahhh!

HOLMES:

They mean nothing.

Watson slumps—

WATSON:

Oh God, Oh, God. *(Watson doubles over, panicking.)*

HOLMES:

And there flops Watson. Panic attacks. Predictable. Ho-hum.

MORIARTY:

Bloody hell, you are a robot.

HOLMES:

I solved the problem of Watson, you know—very recently.

Watson is on the ground. She moans.

HOLMES:
She's incapacitated by genuine pain—

Watson whimpers.

A doctor who can't stand actual suffering! What use is she to me? She should learn to accept—what she is currently capable of!

WATSON:
Nnngh.

Watson is fetal on the ground. Holmes is quite close to Moriarty.

MORIARTY:
(*he prods Watson with his foot*) I must insist you work with me, Holmes— you've got just the right temperament.

HOLMES:
About that. You see the problem is—it's... cheating.

Watson is still on the ground.

MORIARTY:
What?

HOLMES:
Lestrade may be Moriarty—but Moriarty is also Lestrade. Your dependence on externals—your reliance on technology—still renders your work weak and flabby and trite!

Moriarty swings his gun from Watson to Holmes.

MORIARTY:
I beg your pardon.

HOLMES:
You claim we are peers—but no man is my peer! I am an iconoclast, an original, needing no one and nothing but myself! And you're, what—some postmodern digital age *extortionist*? I mean really— hostages, bribery—BLACKMAIL?—it's been *done*!

MORIARTY:
Careful, Holmes—

HOLMES:
You think I want the end of *mystery*?! The process is the *point*, man! The joy of the chase, not control of the hunt! But you never could understand that—for there is no artistic genius in your rotten soul. You're just another petty, pedestrian, posturing criminal; a ho-hum everyday conman, with nothing original to offer! And certainly no match—for me!

She contemptuously tosses her pink gun away, smiling, challenging him

MORIARTY:
I'm about done with this!

HOLMES:
(*triumphant, hopping with glee*) Even that! You have no patience, no rigor—no tolerance for frustration—

MORIARTY:
I rescind my over-generous offer!/

HOLMES:
(*getting more and more energized, manic*) What's more, you violate the key principle in deductive consultation—/

MORIARTY:
/—you are no longer in consideration for the position!!!

HOLMES:
(*more and more*) /Do not project that which you wish is true, but embrace the improbable, and finally—

MORIARTY:
(*he clicks the safety off*) Any last words, Holmes?!!!

HOLMES:
(*triumphant, suddenly still*) Never—jump—to kittens.

MORIARTY:
Kitt /—?

HOLMES:
/NOW

> *The prone Watson suddenly lunges forward and bites Moriarty's ankle HARD—he doubles, yelling, and Holmes grabs the gun*

WATSON:
AAAAAHHHHHHHHHHHHHH

MORIARTY:
AAAAHHHHH

> *The black gun fires, harmlessly, as Holmes grabs it, all yelling desperately—Holmes & Moriarty struggle as Watson jumps off of Moriarty, runs and grabs Holmes' big book and hits Moriarty over the head with it, one, two, three times. The gun goes flying as Moriarty is walloped to his knees:*

WATSON:
AHHHHHHHHHHHHHHHHHH AHHH AHHH AHHH AH!

> *Beat.*

MORIARTY:
—glergh.

107

Moriarty falls flat to the floor, unconscious.

WATSON:

Hnnnnggggh, I'm gonna be sick.

Holmes handcuffs the unconscious Moriarty with Irene's sex cuffs.

HOLMES:

Genuine pain, Moriarty. True suffering. Watson scents it out every time. Her traumatized subconscious was not moved by my fake injuries, nor the dead Mr. Drebber, nor blood at a crime scene. Only other living people's real physical anguish triggers the panic attacks. *(Holmes walks over to Irene)* And she is certainly not—incapacitated by blanks.

Irene pops up.

IRENE:

Sherlock, you've got gunpowder all over my blouse.

WATSON:

Aaaa AAAAAAAAA!

HOLMES:

Watson

WATSON:

AAAAAHHHH

HOLMES:

Watson

WATSON:

AAAAAAHHHHHHHHHHHHHHHHHHHHH WHAT THE FRIG IS FRIGGING HAPPENING

IRENE:

She's hysterical, Sherlock—

WATSON:

WHAT WAS THAT HOW DID THAT WHAT DID YOU HOW

IRENE:

—just let me slap her.

WATSON:

<u>WHAT THE HELL IS GOING ON</u>

HOLMES:

Elementary, my dear—

WATSON:

NO ELEMENTARY NO ELEMENTARY SKIP AHEAD TO THE FRIGGIN EXPOSITION **PLEASE**

HOLMES:
Ahem.
Well. I knew that something was off with "Lestrade" from the beginning. Too much interest in my methods; genuine Scotland Yard men are too busy peacocking around, mansplaining every moment, to ask so many questions. Then there was the incredible coincidence—that this anonymous supergenius popped up right at the same time as the Lieutenant. I had to be sure, of course. So I let him believe he was breadcrumbing me along... as I set the lure of an even bigger trap. *(Holmes picks up her book, waves it smugly.)*—it all became much easier, of course, when Irene signed on.

IRENE:
I, like Sherlock, suspected that there was a mastermind behind certain forces that had intruded upon my life. I made the Monk episode public to attract this purported supergenius's attention, parading a high-level client before the media, so that Moriarty understood my influence. Then when he predictably turned to violence, all I had to do was pretend to wilt into some helpless damsel—"Help me, Sherlock Wan-Kenobi, you're my only hope." *(she laughs)* Please.

HOLMES:
It was all planned right in front of you, Watson. Didn't you catch our many obvious classical allusions?

IRENE:
The "play's the thing to catch the conscience of the king"? From Hamlet, when he lays a trap for his uncle? That's how we decided to make Lestrade reveal himself.

HOLMES:
Or Mario, from *Tosca*? Going to fake execution, when the soldiers used blanks? That's how we planned Irene's staged death.

IRENE:
Or all that talk of Sun Tzu and "joined hands" and "engaging the enemy"? Surely the *Sun Tzu* tipped you off?!!

HOLMES:
Do you really mean to say... that all went... entirely over your head?

WATSON:
.... Well, psht, no, yeah of course I knew that you NO OF COURSE NOT WHY WOULD ANYONE FIGURE OUT ALL OF THIS DOUBLE BLIND SECRET AGENT SPY VERSUS SPY PLAYING THE PLAYER ART OF WAR—BULLHOCKEY? IT'S

ALL JUST SUBTEXT ON SUBTEXT ON SUBTURTLES ALL THE WAY DOWN???!!

IRENE:
—she's cracked.

WATSON:
I'M INSANE? **I'M INSANE?!!!** I'M—WHY? WHY—WHY WOULD YOU EVEN BE INVESTED IN CAPTURING MORIARTY IRENE WHY WOULD YOU WHY WHY CATCH WHY MORIARTY **WHY YOU CATCH WHY MORIARTY WHY WHY WHY WHY WHY WHY WHY WHY WHY WHY**

<u>WHY</u>

IRENE:
I had a personal interest, Watson. Didn't you notice I kept mentioning my *mentor*? And she, of course, was:

HOLMES:
The red-headed woman.

IRENE:
The red-headed *professional*. Left to Moriarty, her killer would have gone free. They do, you know—often.

HOLMES:
And once I knew that you knew that—

IRENE & HOLMES:
(*variously*) I knew that you knew that I knew—

Watson has to struggle not to beat out her brains.

HOLMES:
—well, from then on, it was, child's play.

Beat. Watson chooses to live—barely.

WATSON:
So... it was just—it was lies—it was *all* lies, the—the whole time. No—wait. One thing was true, Holmes, wasn't it? What you said about Irene: but really, you were talking about me. <u>Because I was the bait.</u>

dead serious, close to tears

Right, Sherlock? That's why you keep your hapless little sidekick around—your dupe; the subject of your experiments. (*ready to really kill*) I was just your <u>frigging bait?!!</u>

MORIARTY:
And baited I was! Hook, line, and sinker.

he struggles up

IRENE:
Oh, look who's up.

MORIARTY:
(*he's in a lot of pain, trying to sit up*) Such a—remarkable demonstration, Irene, Sherlock! You are both—truly worth the employ! Now, if you only—let me go—I could arrange compensation beyond your wildest imaginings. Control over—anyone. Power—to create your own—little empires.

HOLMES:
Please, Lestrade-slash-Moriarty. You choked on the carrot, you dropped yer stick—and now you shall face justice.

Irene has begun walking towards Moriarty.

MORIARTY:
Adler—surely we can make a deal! Irene—I can meet your price!!!!

IRENE:
Can you?

Irene has gracefully dropped down and retrieved Moriarty's black gun from the floor.

Dear man—do you recall the Case of the Red-Headed Woman?

HOLMES:
Adler.

She is stalking closer and closer to Moriarty—

IRENE:
None of you ever bothered to even learn her name, did you? My mentor's.

Irene is near Moriarty

HOLMES:
Adler—!

IRENE:
There may be no honor amongst thieves, but there is honor in my profession.
Would you like—to know her name, sir?
It—was—

She FIRES the gun. Moriarty flips over the back of the platform—and is gone.

WATSON:
Blerrgh!

Watson turns away, panicking.

HOLMES:
You *shot* him!

IRENE:
Brilliant deduction, detective.

WATSON:
He's—is he dead?!!!

> *Irene looks over the platform edge.*

IRENE:
That, or he'll have a hell of a wake-up in Bristol. Crash-landed right on the 7:15.

HOLMES:
He was handcuffed! In cold blood, Irene?

IRENE:
In justice, Holmes.

> *She points the black gun at Watson and Holmes.*

IRENE:
Get away from me, gals. This time, they aren't blanks.

HOLMES:
Is this really how you want it to end?

IRENE:
Babe—this is how I want it to continue.
I'll be slipping away into the night now—and taking this naughty little treasure with me.

> *She stoops and grabs Holmes' book.*

Thanks for the retirement plan.

> *She begins to exit.*

HOLMES:
Before you go—I would ask you—to take a look in that book! Of particular interest might be the entry—under Adler, comma, Irene.

IRENE:
For you, dearest? Why not. One last love note for the road!

> *Keeping her gun up—she flips through, awkwardly, looks—looks again—beat—she stares at Sherlock.*

There's—there's nothing here.

WATSON:
What?

IRENE:
>*(enraged)* No—no entries—in the whole thing! Just "All work and no play makes Holmes a dull girl" written over and over again!!! *(she tosses the book away, angrily)*

HOLMES:
>The book wasn't just bait for him, Adler. You were—a most intriguing—mystery. I had to get some answers.
>>*Irene puts up the gun, as Holmes get closer.*

IRENE:
>Stop, Holmes. Stop moving.

HOLMES:
>Give over the gun—you have to face the consequences /

IRENE:
>/STOP IT

HOLMES:
>/Of what you've done—Irene—

IRENE:
>BACK OFF!
>>*Irene has the gun right against Holmes' chest—shaking—*

HOLMES:
>We both know—that you can not hurt me.
>>*Beat. Irene seems like she might really shoot her.*

IRENE:
>Stupid, arrogant Sherlock! I could shoot out that unfeeling heart—if it wouldn't break my own.
>>*Irene drops the gun and suddenly kisses her, HARD. Sherlock freezes—and Irene takes advantage of that to push her into Watson, and runs fast for the platform. Holmes struggles up from the tangle with Watson—and Irene pauses there—looking over:*

HOLMES:
>Irene! No—Don't jump!

IRENE:
>*(Irene smiles.)* What did I say, Watz? Always know how to find the exit.

HOLMES:
>IRENE!
>>*Irene jumps and disappears—they run to the edge—a frozen beat:*

HOLMES:
>My God!—*(a train whistle blows)* Right on top of the 7:20 express!

IRENE (O.S.):
    See you later, ladies! Thanks for all the laughs!
        Irene laughs; it fades as the train whistle blows.
HOLMES:
    Ecco un artista!!! *(Watson looks at her, then slumps down)*
    Well, Watson. One femme fatale, at least two brushes with Death; triple, quadruple, and quintuple-crossing, a good cop who was a bad cop who was a world-not-famous pseudonymous super-villain— *(cheerfully)* A decent night's work—don't you agree?
WATSON:
    —Holmes—I'm moving out.

9.

Back to Apt. 2B. Watson rolls out her little rolly suitcase out. It's awkward.

HOLMES:
Ah, Watson. All—packed up, are you?

WATSON:
Um. I think so. *(re: the bag)* I barely unpacked, to be honest.

HOLMES:
Suppose we were rather busy, the last few months.

Awkward beat.

WATSON:
Well, Holmes.—I guess this is—

HOLMES:
Watson—wait. I wanted you to—to have this.

She hands her the human finger bone.

WATSON:
—it might raise some questions at customs.

HOLMES:
—this, then.

She gives her the kitten puzzle box.

WATSON:
Oh. Okay. Um. Thanks. *(pause)* So—see ya.

Watson begins to roll out.

HOLMES:
Watson—there is—something bothering me. One nagging mystery, yet to be solved.

Watson looks at her

Why are you—leaving?

WATSON:
Look—it really doesn't—*(she stops herself)*—I gotta/ go

HOLMES:

Because—I thought you—rather enjoyed the life! Like—I do. *(Holmes gets in the way as Watson starts to leave)* /And didn't you? Watson, didn't you!

WATSON:

/Holmes—stop, okay, STOP! /You USED me!

HOLMES:

What?

WATSON:

Listen. Last night with Irene and Moriarty, it became clear—that I was playing checkers, and the rest of you are playing chess. I was just, like,—a pawn, in your much bigger game. *(covering for the extremely deep hurt)* And that's... fine, whatever.

But it means—I must just have to find a new place out there—for me in like, the <u>normal</u> world. A world where maybe people aren't so much trying to murder each other over fake blackmail fodder books filled with weird invisible love tests, or whatever.

(A car honks, outside.) Anyway, that must be my cab—

HOLMES:

Did the normal world indeed make a place for you?

WATSON:

What?

HOLMES:

Has that purportedly sane world out there, ever bent to meet your—breakage?

Watson. I've been told, you know,—that I am—heartless. A—robot—remarkable machine.

> *She taps her head.*

But whatever limitations I may have, I am—uniquely suited—designed—for the spheres in which I operate. How could I do my work without detachment? How could I objectively observe with too much feeling clouding my judgment? I make my eccentricities work in my favor. And thus, I see the reason for why they may—exist.

WATSON:

(flatly) So?

HOLMES:

(getting more desperate) So, if there is a me, there must be a counter-me. Somebody who cannot turn off their intense empathy; someone so attuned to other people's suffering that she is, however subconsciously—a kind of human lie detector; able to distinguish

genuine distress from fraud, and feel others' pain—very deeply indeed. A person of that nature might consider—themselves—broken.

But I hypothesize that there is something useful, to be made—with their mixed-up pieces, even if it does not look like the picture on the box.

> *The cab honks again.—Watson opens the door to leave: Holmes, with extreme desperation—*

I—I didn't want you only as my pawn, Watson! In fact, I—depended on you having—moves to make in the game! You know that I have always prided myself on being alone; above all influence. But I find now—that perhaps I <u>have</u> been searching for a real—real—match.

WATSON:
—-Well. Smell you, Nancy Drew.

HOLMES:
That bobby-socked boobie.
Watson—though my book was a ruse—I've been thinking perhaps you should begin to chronicle our adventures, to—connect to—the wider world. On the Twitters, perhaps! Maybe you could even start a true-crime bleg!

WATSON:
A bleg?

HOLMES:
You know. *(she mimes typing, but only with two fingers, like your grandma types)* Typings on the—e-news. Ads and likings and clickers.. A bleg!

WATSON:
A BLOG?
—Maybe you do need me, Holmes.

HOLMES:
So you'll stay on as my mentee?!!!!!!

WATSON:
Not mentee.

HOLMES:
Assistant?

WATSON:
Not assistant.

HOLMES:
—just roommates, then.

WATSON:
Not just roommates. Friends.

HOLMES:
... friends.

They move to shake hands—

WATSON:
If you say the real mystery was the pals we made along the way, I will puke upon your shoes.

There's a ding-dong of the bell—then, a creak on the stairs. Moriarty, in his direct-address narrator mode, has started speaking again... he may cross the stage as he does:

MORIARTY:
Detective stories tell us—there is still hope.

WATSON:
Oh, that's the cabbie—I'll tell him it's off—

MORIARTY:
That solutions can be found, enigmas can be resolved—

HOLMES:
Watson! Don't move!

MORIARTY:
That there is a larger pattern, if we can only—

HOLMES:
That's not a cabbie at all!

MORIARTY:
Focus. Perhaps that is an illusion.

WATSON:
How do you know—wait—

MORIARTY:
Perhaps we can never be sure what game we are playing—

WATSON:
I'm not even going to ask.

MORIARTY:
Let alone if we are losers!

HOLMES:
Surely you can deduce who is coming up the stairs, Watson! The tread, the weight upon each step—even the rhythm of breath!—

MORIARTY:
All we hapless mortals can do is try to fit each piece together—

HOLMES:
It is child's play!

MORIARTY:

—without concentrating overmuch on the final picture.

WATSON:

Of course, no, I totally, totally, totally can predict exactly what is about to happen.

MORIARTY:

Because we never know what is coming next. Let alone—how we fit into the puzzle.

Now, do we?

WATSON:

It is—it is—

MORIARTY:

Yes?

WATSON:

It is—<u>elementary</u>, my dear Holmes.

HOLMES:

Elementary—my dear Watson.

> *Holmes swings the door open—and Irene stands there—*

IRENE:

Ladies, ladies, ladies—

> *Moriarty turns—he is suddenly in the scene, next to Irene in the door— and grins at them:*

MORIARTY:

—do we have a case for you.

END OF PLAY.